Diagram of a gill fungus

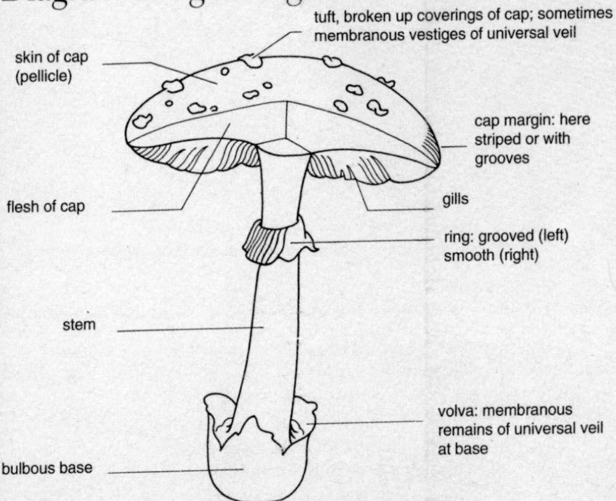

Instruction and warning

This Collins Nature Guide introduces a selection of fungi whose identification features can be recognized with the naked eye. There are 415 species of European fungi shown in colour photographs taken in the field, and each species shown is described in detail. Symbols alongside the mushroom names indicate which species are edible and which are poisonous. Where edible fungi may be confused with poisonous look-alikes, the danger is pointed out in the *similar species* entry.

In order to safely identify any mushroom you have to be certain of every single one of the identifying characteristics given in the description, and match the relevant picture with your find. Even if only one characteristic does not compare, it is best to assume for safety reasons that your f

Eve doubt, you should u n all its different should you collect y th absolute certainty ay very fast.

Alw s identifica ns if you are extremely careful in making positive identifications, and use all the information available. If in slightest doubt, do not eat what you find, or show the fungi you have collected to an expert.

HarperCollins*Publishers*
77–85 Fulham Palace Road
London W6 8JB

98 00 02 01 99 97
2 4 6 8 10 9 7 5 3 1

ISBN 0 00 219994 7

Originally published in German as a GU Nature Guide by
Gräfe und Unzer GmbH, Munich

Reprinted 1996

Written by Edmund Garnweidner
All photographs taken by Edmund Garnweidner
Drawings by Heinz Bogner
This edition translated and adapted by Dr Monika Shaffer-Fehre

Printed and bound in Italy by Officine Grafiche de Agostini, Novara

Collins Nature Guide

MUSHROOMS AND TOADSTOOLS OF BRITAIN & EUROPE

Edmund Garnweidner

Translated and adapted by
DR MONIKA SHAFFER-FEHRE

HarperCollins*Publishers*

Identifying fungi made easy

This Nature Guide is tailor-made for the fungus enthusiast: its convenient pocket-size format and its low weight make it an ideal companion on fungal forays and country rambles.

The colour photographs (taken in the field specially for this book), botanical illustrations and precise, descriptive texts make it easy for anyone to recognize growing fungi and to identify them correctly. The 415 photographs of fungi in the wild show the typical growth form of the mushroom with all the characteristics important for their identification, in their natural surroundings (habitat). The identification of fungi can be difficult for the newcomer, but this book incorporates a system of identification which is as simple as it is practical.

The mushrooms and toadstools are divided into 6 groups each of which is colour coded for simplicity (see p. 6). Coloured thumb markers visible from the book edge make it easy to locate each of the fungal groups. There are symbols in the coloured semi-circles which show the identifying characteristics of each group (see p. 7) which mean that the correct group of mushroom or toadstool can be found easily. Symbols showing at a glance whether the mushroom you have found is EDIBLE or POISONOUS (for explanation of symbols see p. 5) are an important warning. The descriptions warn of poisonous look-alikes (similar species) to edible fungi as well; invaluable information for those who want to gather mushrooms for consumption. The appendix includes some general information on fungi and an index of English and Latin species names. There is also a list of easily identifiable fungi that are particularly good to eat, and hints for their collection and use.

The selection of the fungus species

Besides the fungi of most culinary importance and the poisonous ones, a large percentage of those occurring more frequently in Europe has been mentioned or described under the **similar species** part of the descriptions. Among these are also groups of fungi which have been ignored in some mushroom books.

Colour photographs & descriptions

Each mushroom photograph faces its description, and has the same number. In the descriptions you will find all the important information which will, together with the photograph, make identification possible. The Latin name, according to the most recent botanical nomenclature, is followed by the English common name (when there is one). The characteristic appearance of a fungus is recorded in the following sequence: cap, gills, tubes (pores), stem, flesh, spores and habitat & distribution. All of these aspects are described in detail. In the case of edible fungi, tips for their use are added. In many cases additional information about edibility, content of poison, or any interesting botanical fact is given. Under 'similar species' are included related fungi, those that are of similar appearance and those elsewhere in the book.

The time of year that the fungus is seen is not given for species that fruit during the main fungus season of July to October. The season is included, however, for species which grow earlier or later. The area of distribution of individual fungus species is still too little known and therefore only general statements have been made in this respect.

Symbols used

☺ = Good tasting, edible, recommended for consumption

☠ = Poisonous, not to be eaten, can affect health adversely or is deadly

☒ = Fungi which are endangered or threatened by extinction and which must therefore be totally protected, i.e. not picked.

Important hints for fungi identification

The external characteristics of many fungi are very changeable and cannot always be affirmed beyond doubt.
A safe and exact identification of fungi must rely, therefore, on conscientious and exact observation of every single characteristic. The following rules should be followed carefully.

1) Carefully lift the mushrooms out of the ground and touch them as little as possible; always collect and compare several fruit bodies of different age if available. Individual fruit bodies can often not be easily identified.

2) Once you have found the correct photograph in the Nature Guide, carefully compare every single characteristic of the description with the actual fungus. If even only one characteristic does not fit, you have to assume, as a matter of caution, that you have not found the mushroom described.

3) Only use an edible fungus, even when it has been identified beyond a doubt, when you know all of its developmental stages. This is the only way to protect yourself from being poisoned.

4) Practice makes perfect – start with fungus groups which can be identified more easily (the tube fungi for instance) and practise with species that you are familiar with.

5) If you want to be absolutely certain, have your fungus identifications verified by an expert.

6) Acquaint yourself with the characteristics of the tube fungi and gill fungi which are described and illustrated in the appendix on p. 240 ff. Forms of cap, stem and gills are shown on the inside cover pages. A ruler is also supplied at the front and back of the book, allowing meaurements and size comparisons in the field.

The mushroom groups and colour codes

COLOUR	FUNGUS GROUP	PAGE
	Green covers the boletes and polypores; fungi with distinctly discernible stem and cap, and with a layer of tubes of pores on the underside	8–31
	White covers the gill fungi with a cap, light coloured gills on the underside and a stem without a ring or no stem	32–79
	Violet covers the gill fungi with a cap and distinctly ringed stem	80–101
	Yellow covers the gill fungi with a cap, dark gills and a stem without a ring	102–143
	Blue covers the russulas and lactarias with cap, gills and a stem which has brittle flesh	144–175
	Red covers a wide and varied group of fungi which look different to any of the above groups	176–235

Exceptions to the rule

Fungi with yellow or blue gills have been included with the light or dark gill fungi according to the colour of their spores, white or brown. Species identifications can be confirmed by checking the colour of the spores (see p. 241 on how to make a spore print), which has been given in all individual descriptions of the boletes and gill fungi. The spore test can also be of use in some fungi in which the gills turn brown and blotchy with age, or where the gills darken only when the spores ripen.

Among the gill fungi with a ring there are a number of species in which the ring is indistinct or lost early. In order to avoid incorrectly identifying these mushrooms, many descriptions contain references to similar species, to help ensure that species are not confused.

Symbols used for different fungi shapes

The main colour coded groups above are sub-divided further by the shape and size of the mushroom. This helps to make it quick and easy for each type of mushroom, and then the specific species, to be found in the book. The chart opposite shows the symbols of fungus shapes shown on the thumb tabs on the right hand pages, their defining characteristics, and the pages on which that type of fungi can be found.

SYMBOL	FUNGUS GROUP	PAGE
	Boletes with detachable tube layer	8–27
	Polypores with cap, stem and non-detatchable pores	28–31
	Gill fungi in which the stem is affixed sideways or where it is missing	32–33
	Small gill fungi without a ring, with a cap diameter of less than 5 cm, and stem thickness of less than 8 mm	34–55 102–115
	Larger gill fungi without a ring, cap diameter of more than 5 cm, stem thickness more than 8 mm	56–79 116–143
	Gill fungi, growing singly or in clumps, with a distinct ring	80–101
	Russulas and lactarias with brittle, non-fibrous stem flesh	144–175
	Shelf-like tough or hard fungi, with or without pores, which grow on wood	176–187
	Coral fungi	188–195
	Club fungi	196–197
	Ridged gill fungi	198–199
	Teeth fungi	200–201
	Bovists	202–207
	Earth stars	208–209
	Jelly fungi	212–215
	Sponge and saddle fungi	216–221
	Cup fungi with cup- or bowl-shaped fruit bodies	222–229

1 ## *Boletus edulis* ☺ Cep or Penny-bun

Cap: Hemispherical; pale red- to chestnut-brown, more rarely brown-black, somewhat sticky, shiny; to 20 cm in diameter.
Tubes: Whitish-grey when young, later yellow, olive-green when old; wider near the stem. *Spores:* Olive-brown.
Stem: Marbled pale brownish-red, especially at the tip, with fine, net markings; firm, swollen, bulbous, slender when mature.
Flesh: White, no discolouration; mild, nut-like taste, nice smell.
Habitat & distribution: In coniferous forests particularly below firs and pines; frequent at higher altitudes, becoming scarce due to over collecting, particularly in vicinity of large towns.
Use: Due to pleasant taste suitable for cooking and drying.
Similar species: Can be confused with *Tylopilus felleus* (4).

2 ## *Boletus reticulatus* ☺

Cap: Light buff to grey-brown; mostly dry and velvety, sometimes cracked in patches, otherwise as for Cep (1).
Tubes: Whitish-grey when young, later yellow, olive-green when old. *Spores:* Olive-brown.
Stem: Its reticulate (mesh work) markings can extend to base; when young markings light and stem bulbous; darker and more slender when mature.
Flesh: White, not discolouring, mild taste.
Habitat & distribution: In deciduous woodland, near oaks and beeches, frequently from early summer; not rare.

3 ## *Boletus pinophilus* ☺☒

Cap: Dark chestnut-brown to black-brown, somewhat sticky, shiny, up to 25 cm in diameter, otherwise like the Penny-bun (1).
Tubes: Light grey when young, later yellow, olive-green when old. *Spores:* Olive-brown.
Stem: Dark, red-brown like the cap with distinct, net pattern; compact and club-shaped, later more slender.
Flesh: White, not discolouring; mild taste.
Habitat & distribution: Below pine trees, sometimes silver firs, in N Europe and in mountainous areas; rare but locally in great numbers.

4 ## *Tylopilus felleus* ☠

Cap: Hemispherical; yellow- or reddish-brown; matt and downy, slightly slippery; mostly 6-10 cm, rarely above 20 cm in diameter.
Tubes: Young greyish-white, then pale pink. *Spores:* Pinkish-brown.
Stem: Mostly long and slender with a swollen, bulbous base and a coarse, deeply alveolate, dark net.
Flesh: White, not discolouring; very bitter taste.
Habitat & distribution: In coniferous forests, usually common; when immature often similar to Cep (1), distinguished by a dark net on the stem and tubes which turn pink later. *Tylopilus felleus* can also be distinguished by its bitter taste. It contains small, harmless amounts of the fungal poison muscarin; it may cause stomach upsets and is inedible.

1

left
2
right
3

4

5 ## *Boletus queletii* ☺☒

Cap: Hemispherical, flattening out when older; as in *Boletus luridus* (7) olive- or reddish-brown, rarely also dark red.
Tubes: Yellow, turning blue where cut; pores golden yellow to orange-red. *Spores:* Olive.
Stem: Pale golden yellow, often more slender and redder towards the base; smooth, though minutely puberulous spots apparent under a lens.
Flesh: Yellow, almost white when old; at base of stem mostly wine- to blood-red turning blue; slightly acid taste.
Habitat & distribution: Scarce; in deciduous forests, mostly under beeches, not at high altitudes; edible, but should be protected.

6 ## *Boletus erythropus* ☺

Cap: Hemispherical when young, then bolster-like, curved or flat; dark grey to black-brown; finely felty, slippery when wet.
Tubes: Yellow, later olive; immediately black-blue on cutting.
Spores: Olive-brown.
Stem: Slender with obese, bulbous base; orange-yellow covered densely by tiny, carmine tufts; turning blue-black when bruised.
Flesh: Yellow, immediately dark blue on cutting, turning pale again later, mild taste.
Habitat & distribution: In deciduous woodland and in pine forests particularly with bilberries, more frequent at higher altitudes.
Use: For cooking and frying, not suitable for freezing.

7 ## *Boletus luridus* ☠

Cap: Hemispherical when young, then convex to almost flat; light olive-brown, sometimes with yellow or pink hues; to 20 cm in diameter.
Tubes: Yellow when young, olive when old; pores orange-red, turning green-blue when bruised, with a wine-red line in the flesh of the cap above. *Spores:* Olive-brown.
Stem: Fairly slender with a club-shaped base; lemon- to orange-yellow with long extended, reddish-brown mesh which, when old, is dark greyish-brown, turning deep blue when bruised.
Flesh: Yellow, dark red at base of stem, turning blue when cut, but becoming paler after some time, mild taste.
Habitat & distribution: From June in deciduous and coniferous forests. Frequent under beeches.
Use: This fungus is often eaten, but can have a slightly toxic effect when cooked insufficiently.
This fungus contains a trace of the fungal poison muscarin in non-active quantities. The blue colouration of the flesh occurs in many tube fungi and not an indication of edibility of any given fungus.

5

6

7

8 *Boletus satanas* ☠

Cap: Evenly hemispherical to convex when young, later often contorted and flattened; at first grey, later greyish-yellow to light buff-ochre; can be more than 25 cm in diameter.
Tubes: Yellow; pores soon orange to deep carmine, becoming greenish-blue when bruised. *Spores:* Olive.
Stem: Short, firm, club-shaped, the lower half is yellow with a carmine hue, rarely entirely red or yellow; the top half is patterned by a mesh.
Flesh: Yellowish-white, turning slowly blue when cut; initially without scent, but older fruiting bodies smell unpleasantly of carrion.
Habitat & distribution: Under beech trees on chalk, mainly in sunny spots; rare, but can be locally frequent; not dangerously poisonous, but causes stomach and abdominal disorders which may persist for several days.

9 *Boletus rhodoxanthus* ☠ ☒

Cap: Initially convex, soon bolster-shaped; at the apex mostly whitish-grey to pale buff, slowly flushing a beautiful pink from the margin; can exceed 20 cm in diameter.
Tubes: Yellow, yellowish-green when old, turning blue when cut.
Spores: Olive to dark carmine.
Stem: Bulbous only when young, then rather slender; a dense, narrow, carmine mesh over a yellow base colour.
Flesh: Bright lemon yellow, immediately turning blue when cut; mild taste.
Habitat & distribution: In warm, deciduous forests on chalk, mainly under oak and beech; rare; edible, but because of its rarity should not be collected; possibly the most colourful European fungus.
Similar species: Boletus splendidus grows in similar habitat, but is of a generally darker colour; its cap is initially mouse grey and flushes later carmine to wine-red from the rim.

10 *Boletus rhodopurpureus* ☠

Cap: Cushion-like (pulvinate); grey or greyish-brown when young, later flushing red or dark purple from the rim; up to 12 cm in diameter.
Tubes: At first yellow when cut, then turning dark blue; pores deep purple. *Spores:* Olive-brown.
Stem: Usually slender, but rather short relative to the cap; occasionally very bulbous. Dark yellow background overlaid by dark blood-red, very dense mesh.
Flesh: Pale yellow, turning blue when cut.
Habitat & distribution: In coniferous forests mostly near silver fir or spruce on chalk, mainly at higher altitude.
Similar species: In the warmest regions of central Europe and in southern Europe the dark, blood-red *Boletus dupainii*.

8

9

10

11 *Boletus calopus* ☠

Cap: Broad, cushion-like, light olive-grey, later light grey-brown; up to 15 cm in diameter.
Tubes: Light yellow, olive when old, blue when bruised, narrow.
Spores: Light olive-ochre.
Stem: Bulbous club-shaped, but also slender; in the lower part strongly carmine, otherwise yellow with a minute mesh pattern
Flesh: Yellowish-white, turning deep blue when cut, mostly bitter, occasionally has a mild taste.
Habitat & distribution: Frequent in pine forests and deciduous forests, mainly at higher altitudes; inedible due to its bitter taste; causes stomach and abdominal pains.

12 *Boletus radicans* ☠☒

Cap: Evenly convex, very fleshy, pale grey, buff when old, epidermis of cap extending beyond rim, up to 15 cm in diameter.
Tubes: Lemon-yellow, blue when bruised; narrow pores. *Spores:* Olive.
Stem: Short and bulbous, rarely also club-shaped; lemon-yellow at the apex with a narrow one-coloured mesh; has a short attenuate root-like appendix at the base.
Flesh: Yellowish-white, turning blue when cut, rather bitter, so inedible.
Habitat & distribution: Under oak and copper beech on chalk often together with *Boletus satanas*, very rare so should be protected.
Similar species: The very rare *Boletus impolitus* grows under oak and is deceptively similar in colour but has a more slender stem without mesh and flesh with a mild taste.

13 *Boletus fechtneri* ☺☒

Cap: Initially convex, then cushion-shaped; silver-grey, later somewhat buff-ochre; up to 15 cm in diameter.
Tubes: Light yellow as in *Boletus radicans* (12). *Spores:* Olive.
Stem: As in *B. radicans*, yellow with minute mesh of the same colour, but frequently with carmine hue around middle of stem; not rooting.
Flesh: Yellowish-white, turning green to green-blue when cut; mild taste.
Habitat & distribution: In warm, deciduous forests on chalk, occasionally together with other rare tube fungi; rare, so should not be collected despite its good taste.

14 *Gyrodon lividus* ☺☒

Cap: Convex when young, later flat and strongly contorted; initially straw-coloured, then a dingy grey-brown and staining with deep-brown blotches, slippery; up to 15 cm in diameter, but usually less.
Tubes: A beautiful lemon-yellow, deeply decurrent on the stem, immediate black-blue discolouration when touched. *Spores:* Brown.
Stem: Slender and cylindrical with attenuated base; yellow with dull reddish-brown blotches.
Flesh: Yellowish-white, turning deep blue when cut, very soft in the cap.
Habitat & distribution: Only below alders, mostly in moist localities, forms fairy rings occasionally.

11

left
12
right
13

14

15 *Xerocomus badius* ☺ Bay Bolete

Cap: Convex when young, later flat; dark chestnut-brown; minutely velvety, slippery in moist weather; mostly 8-12 cm, rarely up to 25 cm in diameter.
Tubes: Pale greenish-yellow when young, soon pale green, olive when old, turning blue-green when bruised. *Spores:* Olive-brown.
Stem: Slender, but occasionally bulbous; marbled chestnut-brown on a dirty yellow background, no mesh, flesh firm.
Flesh: Yellowish-white, turning blue slowly when cut, becoming pale again after some time, mild taste.
Habitat & distribution: In coniferous forests, particularly at higher altitudes below spruce and pine; very frequent.
Use: Suitable for all recipes, though slimy when cooked; good for seasoning.
Similar species: Xerocomus spadiceus has bright golden-yellow tubes and a coarse, longitudinally ribbed stem and is probably only a particular growth form of *Xerocomus subtomentosus*.

16 *Xerocomus subtomentosus* ☺ Downy Bolete

Cap: Convex, flat when old; light olive-brown; minutely felty, never slippery; up to 10 cm in diameter.
Tubes: A beautiful chrome-yellow, can become blue when bruised, but mostly unchanged; pores wide. *Spores:* Brownish-olive.
Stem: Long and slender; marbled pale reddish-brown.
Flesh: Pale yellow, often turning blue, mild taste.
Habitat & distribution: On acid soil in pine forests usually close to bilberry, wide distribution.
Use: Recommended equally for cooking, frying and drying.

17 *Xerocomus chrysenteron* ☺ Red-cracked Bolete

Cap: Convex, later flat and contorted; dark olive-brown when young, soon becoming light grey-brown and cracked in areola, pale cherry-red where wounded; minutely velvety or pruinose; up to 8 cm in diameter.
Tubes: Light yellow, blue when bruised; pores wide. *Spores:* Olive-brown.
Stem: Long and slender; light yellow, often with cherry-red colouration, particularly around the middle of the stem, sometimes with red tufts (flocci) which can be pure yellow in autumn forms.
Flesh: Light yellow, sometimes turning blue; cap soft and fast decaying.
Habitat & distribution: Deciduous and coniferous forests; frequent.
Use: Young fungi are palatable and suitable for drying, but they become slimy when cooked; mature specimens are tasteless and decay quickly.

18 *Xerocomus rubellus* ☺

Cap: In size and form resembling *X.chrysenteron*, but bright cherry-red.
Tubes: Pale yellow, as in *X. chrysenteron*. *Spores:* Olive-brown.
Stem: Pale yellow, sometimes with reddish colours or tufts.
Flesh: Yellow, soft, usually turning blue when cut.
Habitat & distribution: In deciduous and mixed forests; in groups and often together with *X. chrysenteron* (17); but fairly rare.

15

left
16
right
17

18

19 *Boletus piperatus* ☠ **Peppery Bolete**

Cap: Convex; coppery red-brown; sticky when wet; up to 6 cm in diameter.
Tubes: Coppery red-brown; wide pores. *Spores:* Cinnamon-brown.
Stem: Slender; coppery red-brown.
Flesh: In the cap pale red-brown, in the stem sulphur-yellow; very hot scent.
Habitat: Frequent in pine forests.
Use: Powderized for seasoning.

20 *Xerocomus parasiticus* ☠☒ **Parasitic Bolete**

Cap: Hemispherical, then flat; yellowish-brown, later darker; felty (tomentose); to 5 cm in diameter.
Tubes: Pale yellow, later light olive-brown. *Spores:* Dark olive.
Stem: Pale yellow or olive; with some tufts.
Flesh: Pale yellow; mild taste.
Habitat: Only on decaying potato bovists, rare, should be protected.

21 *Boletus pulverulentus* ☺

Cap: Convex, flat when old; dark red-brown, becoming lighter with age; minutely felty, not slippery; up to 8 cm in diameter.
Tubes: Light to olive-yellow, turning blue-black on contact. *Spores:* Olive.
Stem: Long and slender; yellow or red-brown, tufted.
Flesh: Yellow, immediately turning blue-black when cut, mild taste.
Habitat & distribution: In deciduous and mixed forests, particularly near beech and oak; fairly rare.

22 Suillus variegatus ☺

Cap: Convex to flat; light yellow-brown; felty and grainy, to 10 cm in diameter.
Tubes: Olive-yellow with dark olive-brown, narrow pores. *Spores:* Olive.
Stem: Ochre to orange-yellow blotchy and minutely felty.
Flesh: Yellowish, becoming weakly blue when cut, mild taste.
Habitat & distribution: Found only under pines, particularly on sandy soil with bilberries; frequent.

23 *Gyroporus castaneus* ☺☒

Cap: Convex, soon flat; yellow- to ochre-brown; velvety; to 8 cm in diameter.
Tubes: White, soon pale yellow with brown blotches; sinuate. *Spores:* Yellow.
Stem: Slender; red-brown and velvety; later hollow. *Flesh:* White, mild.
Habitat & distribution: In deciduous and pine forests, in meadows, only on soils with minimal lime content; rare, should be protected.

24 *Pulveroboletus gentilis* ☺☒

Cap: Hemispherical to convex; light reddish-brown, also meat-pink or cherry-red; moistly sticky; only 2-4 cm in diameter.
Tubes: Bright chrome yellow, pores very wide. *Spores:* Olive.
Stem: Yellow, reddish-brown in places, somewhat slippery.
Flesh: Yellowish-white; mild taste.
Habitat & distribution: In deciduous forests, also at the base of living trees; rare and should be protected.

left
19
right
20
left
21
right
22
left
23
right
24

25 *Suillus grevillei* ☺ Larch Bolete

Cap: Convex when young, later spreading, flat when old; bright orange- or red-brown, more rarely yellow; very slippery, with soft flesh, up to 12 cm in diameter.
Tubes: Pale yellow, later olive-yellow; with very narrow pores; adnate.
Spores: Olive-yellow to golden-brown.
Stem: Slender; orange-brown like the cap; with weak mesh at the apex; first a slimy yellow ring covers the tubes; it disappears later.
Flesh: Light yellow throughout; very watery; mild taste.
Habitat & distribution: Only under larches, mainly at higher altitudes, often occurring in great numbers.

26 *Suillus viscidus* ☺

Cap: Hemispherical when young, later convex to flat; whitish-grey, then darker, blotchy when old, slimy; up to 12 cm in diameter.
Tubes: White, later grey, blotchy (epichroic) when bruised; pores wider than in *Suillus grevillei* often serrate at opening, adnate or somewhat decurrent. *Spores:* Clay-coloured.
Stem: Greyish-yellow; with a hint of a slimy ring that often cannot be seen on the mature fungus.
Flesh: Whitish-grey, within the stem also yellowish then turning slightly grey; very soft; mild taste.
Habitat & distribution: Only under larches, mainly at high altitudes; often together with *Suillus grevillei,* but not as frequent.

27 *Suillus tridentinus* ☺

Cap: Convex; orange to rusty red, more rarely yellow; stickily slimy and often covered with dark-brown scales or fibrils; up to 12 cm in diameter.
Tubes: Yellow when young, later bright orange; adnate to the stem; pores with distinctly wider openings than S. *grevillei*. *Spores:* Brownish-olive.
Stem: Slender, a rusty-orange like the cap; with a hint of a slimy, yellowish-white ring that soon disappears.
Flesh: Lemon-yellow; mild taste.
Habitat & distribution: Only under larches, at higher altitudes on chalk; together with larch boletes (25), but more scarce.

28 *Boletinus cavipes* ☺

Cap: Convex when young, later flat and often with a small boss; chestnut-brown, felty and scaly, more rarely also yellow; up to 12 cm in diameter.
Tubes: Yellow when young, later light olive-green. Pores very wide and quite noticeably dentate; with radiating cross walls that continue from rim of cap to top of stem, decurrent. *Spores:* Olive-ochre.
Stem: Yellow at the apex, chestnut-brown like the cap below, scaly; with a weak ring which is not seen on older fungi; hollow.
Flesh: Pale yellow; scentless, mild taste.
Habitat & distribution: Only under larches; frequent at higher altitudes, elsewhere more scarce.

25

left
26
right
27

28

29 *Suillus placidus* ☺☒

Cap: Hemispherical when young, later convex; ivory white; very slimy, with soft flesh; up to 10 cm in diameter.
Tubes: Pale whitish-grey when young, mostly with milk white drops, later pale lemon yellow; adnate, pores narrow. *Spores:* Dingy ochre.
Stem: Slender; ivory white, with greyish-violet blotches and dots near the top; no ring.
Flesh: Yellowish-white; mild taste.
Habitat & distribution: On high mountains beneath Swiss stone pine (*Pinus cembra*) but also on lower ground under planted yellow pines (*P. strobus*); rare, should be protected.

30 *Suillus luteus* ☺ Slippery Jack

Cap: Hemispherical when young, later convex, can be flat when old; deep chocolate-brown, more rarely yellowish- or greyish-brown; very slimy, rather marbled and shiny when dry; mostly 6-10 cm in diameter.
Tubes: Pale yellowish when young and pale greenish-yellow when old; no discolouration on bruising; pores narrow; adnate. *Spores:* Rusty-brown.
Stem: Apex yellowish with dark dots; below the broad, greyish-violet ring there is a slimy cover which is brown when old; the ring fades with age.
Flesh: White when young, yellowish when old; cap soft and watery; mild taste.
Habitat & distribution: Only below pines, often together with other tube fungi specific to pines.

31 *Suillus granulatus* ☺ Granulated Boletus

Cap: Initially hemispherical, later convex or flat; light yellow- to orange-brown; very slimy, with soft flesh; up to 10 cm in diameter.
Tubes: Pale yellow and often with milky drops when young, then light yellowish-olive or brown; pores narrow; mostly adnate. *Spores:* Yellow-ochre.
Stem: Yellowish-white, no ring; with water droplets when young, later with darker spots.
Flesh: Yellowish-white, not discolouring; very soft; mild taste.
Habitat & distribution: Under various species of pine; communial and frequently in large groups.

32 *Suillus bovinus* ☺ Shallow pored Bolete

Cap: Convex when young, later flat and often irregularly contorted, occasionally funnel-shaped; coppery red-brown; very slippery; mostly 3-6 cm, rarely over 10 cm in diameter.
Tubes: Greyish-yellow when young, later copper-coloured, olive when old; with noticeably irregular, wide pores, the pores have toothed edges when old; adnate or somewhat decurrent. *Spores:* Pale to olive-brown.
Stem: Similar colour as the cap; minutely scaly, later bare; no ring.
Flesh: Pale yellow or brownish, often turning red when cut.
Habitat & distribution: Only below pines, often in large groups and not infrequently in clumps; predominantly at forest fringes, along forest paths and often in fens.

29

left
30

right
31

32

33 *Leccinum scabrum* ☺ Birch Bolete

Cap: Hemispherical when young, later usually evenly convex; varies from pale grey to greyish-brown to dark mouse-grey, occasionally reddish-brown; rather thick flesh, soft when old; surface minutely felty when young and rather slippery when moist; up to 12 cm in diameter.
Tubes: Whitish-grey when young, later greyish-brown; not blotching when bruised; sinuate in vicinity of stem. *Spores:* Brown.
Stem: Whitish-grey; covered entirely with pale grey scales; rather long and slender, base slightly thicker.
Flesh: Whitish-grey, occasionally pink when cut or turning greenish-blue particularly at the base of the stem; without scent; mild taste.
Habitat & distribution: Only under birches, within woods or at their fringe; mostly frequent.
Use: Young mushrooms with firm flesh are very palatable, but they turn grey and rather slimy when cooked. Drying not recommended.

34 *Leccinum griseum* ☺

Cap: Convex; usually greyish-brown, but can be light or olive-brown; with fine bloom and often has small furrows and pits; up to 15 cm in diameter.
Tubes: As the birch bolete (33); light greyish-brown, dirty yellowish-grey when old. *Spores:* Tobacco-brown.
Stem: As the birch bolete, but mostly with longitudinal furrows.
Flesh: Dingy white, slowly turning grey-violet when cut, particularly in the stem; mild taste.
Habitat & distribution: Only below hornbeam, mostly in small groups, not rare.
Use: As for birch bolete.

35 *Leccinum quercinum* ☺

Cap: In form and colour very similar to the orange birch bolete (36), but with orange-red to apricot-yellow shades; up to 25 cm in diameter.
Tubes: White when young, later grey or greyish-yellow. *Spores:* Brown.
Stem: As the Orange Birch Bolete, but with small orange-brown scales which turn reddish-brown and almost black with age.
Flesh: Whitish-grey, turning reddish when cut, finally becoming greyish-violet.
Habitat & distribution: Only below oak, rather rare.
Similar species: Leccinum rufum with a cap which is a lighter orange-brown and has copper-coloured scales on the stem; occurs only under poplar and aspen.

36 *Leccinum versipelle* ☺ Orange Birch Bolete

Cap: Broadly convex, bright red-brown, brick-red or orange-brown; minutely felty, pellicle arches over rim, up to 20 cm in diameter.
Tubes: Whitish-grey at first, later light grey-ochre, sinuate. *Spores:* Brown.
Stem: Small black scales on a white stem; mostly long and slender, can be club-like at base when old; flesh firm.
Flesh: White to pink; turning green-blue when cut, particularly in the stem.
Habitat & distribution: Only below birch, often with birch bolete; frequent.
Use: Turns black when cooked.

33

left
34
right
35

36

37 *Strobilomyces strobilaceus* ☠

Cap: Initially convex, later flat; dark, greyish-brown to almost black; densely covered with broad, very soft, grey, black-tipped scales which are upright at the apex and overlaid like tiles towards the margin; grey and very woolly at the margin when young; mostly 6-12 cm, rarely over 20 cm in diameter.
Tubes: Whitish-grey, discolouring darkly when bruised; pores large.
Spores: Black; spores spherical with a reticulate surface pattern, in contrast to the spores of all other tube fungi which are elliptical or narrowly fusiform.
Stem: Grey, woolly and scaly, turning blackish-grey when bruised; long and slender, very firm.
Flesh: Whitish-grey, discolouring to dirty-reddish or blackish-grey when bruised.
Habitat & distribution: Mostly single in deciduous woodland and coniferous forests, rather rare.

38 *Porphyrellus porphyrosporus* ☠

Cap: Hemispherical when young, later convex to almost flat; light grey when young, soon dark tobacco-brown to light greyish-brown; surface matt and smooth, not slippery, substantially fleshy; mostly 8-14 cm in diameter.
Tubes: Light greyish-yellow when young, soon greyish-brown, becoming blotchy when bruised; tubes lower in vicinity of stem; pores mostly narrow, but occasionally wide in which case the pores reach up to the surface of the cap. *Spores:* Dark reddish.
Stem: Like the cap, dark tobacco-brown to black-brown and minutely velvety; rather slender and thin.
Flesh: White, turning weakly greenish-blue when cut, particularly above the tubes, otherwise slowly reddening, mainly under the pellicle; scentless and with mild taste.
Habitat & distribution: Mostly in small groups in deciduous woodlands and in coniferous forests, particularly frequent at higher altitudes.
Similar species: The fungus has no look-alikes, but recently it has been split into two species. A lighter species with slowly reddening flesh grows in deciduous lowland forests, whilst a darker form whose flesh turns blue above the pores is supposed to occur in coniferous mountain forests. Both forms, however, are often found together and their flesh sometimes turns first blue and then reddish. Therefore it is not often possible to distinguish bewteen the two forms. *Porphyrellus porphyrosporus* and *Strobilomyces strobilaceus* have spores that distinguish them from other fungi and pigments with a different chemical makeup from that of other tube fungi. They are therefore seen as an individual family, the Strobilomycetaceae.

37

38

39 *Polyporus squamosus* ☠ Dryad's saddle

Cap: Depressed when young, with inrolled margin, flat funnel-shaped when old; broad dark-red to chestnut-brown scales cover a background of light ochre; up to over 60 cm in diameter.
Pores: White; wide opening, deeply anchored in the flesh of the cap and therefore cannot be detached. *Spores:* White.
Stem: Usually sideways, dark brown to black at the base, cream-coloured above, with mesh marking, very short and condensed.
Flesh: White; rather soft initially, later hard.
Habitat & distribution: From May to September on living or dead trunks and stumps of various broad-leaved trees, mostly in larger groups, likes sunny spots mainly at forest fringes and on free standing trees.

40 *Polyporus leptocephalus* ☠

Cap: Convex when young, soon flat and mostly of irregular shape; red-brown when young, greyish-yellow when old; bare and smooth; mostly 2-5 cm in diameter.
Pores: White, slightly brown when bruised; very narrow. *Spores:* White.
Stem: As the cap, light reddish-brown or yellowish-brown with a black base; often affixed a little sideways.
Habitat & distribution: On the branches of broad-leaved trees.
Similar species: There are two other polypores with an entirely black stem, *Polyporus badius* with shiny red-brown to purple-black cap up to 20 cm across, and the dark brown, velvety *Polyporus melanopus,* which is 10 cm across and found on dead roots and wood of broad-leaved trees.

41 *Polyporus brumalis* ☠ Winter polypore

Cap: First convex, later expanded or funnel-shaped; hazel to greyish-brown; felty, scaly, becoming bare when old; mostly 4-8 cm in diameter.
Pores: White to pale straw-colour; very narrow, decurrent, cannot be detached. *Spores:* White.
Stem: Pale greyish-brown, faintly marbled, not black at the base.
Flesh: White, very tough, mild taste.
Habitat & distribution: On the wood of various broad-leaved trees; from November to April.
Similar species: Polyporus lepideus has darker cap and stem and very much narrower pores. It grows in early summer on stumps of broad-leaved trees. *Polyporus ciliatus* grows on twiglets of broad-leaved trees has very tiny pores that can only be discerned with a lens.

42 *Polyporus mori* ☠ ☒

Cap: Light ochre-brown and with minute scales like the winter polypore.
Pores: White, noticeably wide, 2-5 mm in size, honeycomb-like and very stretched; often comparable to gills near the stem. *Spores:* White.
Stem: Light grey, scaly like the winter polypore (41).
Habitat & distribution: On branches of broadleaved trees, only in warmer regions; rather rare and should be protected.

39

left
40
right
41

42

43 *Polyporus umbellatus* ☠

Fruitbody: Composed of numerous, often several hundred, caps. They are 1-4 cm in diameter, deeply umbilicate, brown, minutely scaly and form the extremities of a strong, many-branched stock; the compound fungus is up to 40 cm in diameter and weighs several kilogrammes.
Pores: White, narrow.
Stock: Whitish-grey; it originates from a thick, hard, tuber-like nodule (sclerotium) deep underground.
Flesh: White; rather soft when young and later tough.
Habitat & distribution: On roots of old beeches and oaks, often several metres distant from stem; often still growing for many years around the stump after a tree has been felled; rather rare.

44 *Onnia tomentosa* ☠

Cap: Flat when young, with blunt, rounded and light yellowish-white margin, later with slightly depressed centre and contorted in a wave pattern towards the rim, which has a rather sharp edge when old; covered in felt which is light greyish-brown when young and more rusty-brown at maturity; without circular zones, up to 10 cm in diameter.
Pores: Light grey and weakly angular, rather short, anchored only 1-2 mm deep in the flesh of the cap, somewhat decurrent.
Stem: Dark brown to almost black; minutely felty (tomentose), short and thick, often affixed sideways.
Flesh: Ochre-brown under the cap surface, below that yellowish; very hard and fibrous, two layers within the cap.
Habitat & distribution: In coniferous forests, mostly in large groups and frequently merging with the caps of neighbouring fruitbodies; rather frequent at higher altitudes, more rare on lower ground.
Similar species: Coltricia perennis is very similar, but has a weakly circularly zoned, later bare, cap; flesh of cap stained uniformly.

45 *Scutiger ovinus* ☺☒

Cap: Convex when young, soon irregularly contorted; greyish-white when young, soon with yellowish or pale buff hues; up to 6 cm in diameter.
Pores: White when young, yellowing when old, very narrow.
Stem: White, rather short, evenly thick and with rather firm flesh; gradually widening into cap.
Flesh: White when young, later staining lemon yellow, particularly in the stem; still rather soft when young, but soon tough, mild taste, pleasant smell of almonds.
Habitat & distribution: In large groups in coniferous forests; rather frequent, mainly at higher altitudes.
Similar species: Scutiger confluens is larger, mostly gathers in clumps and its cap is light orange from the start.

43

44

45

46 *Pleurotus ostreatus* ☺ Oyster Mushroom

Cap: Shell-shaped with long inrolled margin; dark grey to steel blue when young, later paling to light buff; smooth, with felted margin; to 12 cm in diameter.
Gills: White or light grey; narrow and very crowded, often forked at the base and decurrent. *Spores:* White.
Stem: White; off centre, short and thick, shaggy.
Flesh: White, without scent, mild taste.
Habitat & distribution: In dense clusters on stumps or living trunks of various deciduous trees, more rarely on pine; October to March; in most areas fairly rare; though grows easily on wood.
Use: Suitable for frying and stewing; not for drying.

47 *Panellus mitis* ☠ Kidney-shaped Pleurotus.

Cap: Shell- to kidney-shaped with long inrolled margin; pure white when young, later occasionally reddish-brown; thin flesh has rubber-like skin which can be pulled off; to 2 cm in diameter.
Gills: White, narrow and crowded. *Spores:* White.
Stem: White, somewhat scaly and fibrous; excentric; very short and stout, widening at the base.
Flesh: White, without scent, no taste.
Habitat & distribution: On thin branches of various conifers, very frequent; predominantly from November to February.
Similar species: Crepidotus variabilis is distinguished by light, rust-brown gills and the almost complete lack of a stem. It grows on branches of deciduous trees during summer and autumn.

48 *Schizophyllum commune* ☠ Split Gill

Cap: Shell-shaped; tissue concentrated at point of attachment, resembling a stem; often wavy and lobed, margin ridged when old; very tough, felted and hairy, slippery when moist; reddish-brown and indistinctly zonated, greyish-white when dry; to 4 cm in diameter.
Gills: Pale reddish- or purplish-grey; very narrow with longitudinally split edge which becomes inrolled when wet; the only known fungus with split gills, that are capable of reacting by movement.
Habitat & distribution: Throughout the year on dead deciduous and coniferous wood, predominately from late autumn to spring; very frequent.

49 *Panellus serotinus* ☠ Yellowish Pleurotus

Cap: Hemispherical when young, soon shell-shaped and later often irregularly lobed, fleshy; often a lovely yellow when young, soon dark olive-green; minutely velvety over a jelly-like layer; mostly up to 5 cm, rarely to 10 cm in diameter.
Gills: White, yellow at maturity; narrow and crowded. *Spores:* White.
Stem: Orange-yellow, later orange-brown; minutely velvety, spotted, with felted base; thick and short.
Habitat & distribution: From November on stumps and fallen trunks of various deciduous trees; rarely also on conifer wood; fairly frequent.

46

left
47
right
48

49

50 *Laccaria amethystea* ☺ Amethyst Deceiver

Cap: Broadly convex or funnel-shaped; beautifully amethyst or violet when young, light whitish-grey when dry; minutely scaly; to 5 cm in diameter.
Gills: Amethyst-violet, thick and noticeably distant. *Spores:* White.
Stem: Amethyst-violet, with silky, fibrous overlay; long and slender.
Flesh: Violet, mild taste.
Habitat & distribution: Frequent in deciduous and coniferous forests.

51 *Laccaria laccata* ☺ The Deceiver

Distinguished from the Amethyst Deceiver (50) only by its uniformly flesh-pink colouration. *Laccaria proxima* is also flesh-pink but is larger and grows in fens. *L. bicolor* is pale blue at the stem base and its gills are lilac-blue.

52 *Lepiots castanea* ☠

Cap: Broadly bell-shaped to flat; dark red-brown; soon splitting and minutely scaly; to 3 cm in diameter.
Gills: White; crowded. *Spores:* White.
Flesh: White, mild taste.
Stem: Dark chestnut-brown, floccose on light reddish-brown skin.
Habitat & distribution: In deciduous and coniferous woodlands, mostly singly or in small groups; fairly rare.
This fungus is dangerously poisonous. It may contain traces of amanitin, the poison of the bulbous agaric. Compare fungi of p. 89 and p. 91.

53 *Lepiota clypeolaria* ☠

Cap: Egg-shaped when young, soon broadly bell-shaped and often bluntly umbonate; dark straw-brown; dissolved into small scales at the margin; to 5 cm, rarely up to 8 cm in diameter.
Gills: White; crowded. *Spores:* White.
Stem: White; rather long and slender with indistinct fringed ring-zone when young; white and coarsely woolly; hollow.
Flesh: White, with an unpleasant, stinging smell.
Habitat & distribution: In deciduous forests, frequent. Compare p. 89.

54 *Cystolepiota bucknallii* ☠

Cap: At first conical, later convex to flat; minutely flaky and grainy; blue-violet or whitish-grey; to 3 cm in diameter.
Gills: White, crowded. *Spores:* White.
Flesh: White; with strong smell of coal gas.
Stem: Blue-violet, purple when bruised, long, slender, no ring, often contorted.
Habitat & distribution: In moist beech forests; fairly rare.

55 *Cystolepiota seminuda* ☠

Cap: Convex or bell-shaped; white, evenly minutely grainy; margin often fringed; to 2 cm in diameter.
Gills: White; crowded. *Spores:* White.
Stem: White, discolouring purple when bruised; flaky and grainy.
Habitat & distribution: On humus, along forest roads, frequent.

left
50
right
51

left
52
right
53

left
54
right
55

56 *Clitocybe dealbata* ☠ Ivory Clitocybe

Cap: Convex with inrolled margin when young, later expanded with depressed centre, often contorted, more rarely funnel-shaped; white, glossy, can be dirty buff when old; 2-4 cm in diameter.
Gills: White, can be pale cream when old; narrow, thin and crowded, decurrent when old, otherwise adnate. *Spores:* White.
Stem: Off-white; evenly thick or attenuated towards base, slender and rather long, often flattened, minutely pruinose at apex.
Flesh: White; with distinctly mealy smell.
Habitat & distribution: On grass along waysides, on slopes, occasionally in domestic gardens; mostly in large groups, sometimes fused with one another.
Clitocybe dealbata contains large amounts of the fungal poison muscarin; it has reportedly caused fatalities.
Similar species: Clitocybe rivulosa grows in similar habitats and is distinguished by a cap that is light flesh-brownish, with a white bloom and has concentric cracking on the surface when old. Distinguishing this also very poisonous fungus is not easy; some experts regard it just as one form of *C. dealbata*. On beech litter, more rarely needle litter, grows the larger, also poisonous *C. candicans* with characteristically geniculate stem-base. There are several more, larger clitocybes of which some are poisonous. None should be tasted.

57 *Lyophyllum connatum* ☠

Cap: When young, convex with inrolled wavy, notched and pruinose margin, later irregularly domed and contorted; dirty, off-white; mostly 3-7 cm, occasionally also over 10 cm in diameter.
Gills: Cream-white; crowded, initially adnate or sinuate, later somewhat decurrent. *Spores:* White.
Stem: Dirty-white, floccose when young; evenly thick.
Flesh: Off-white; with rancid, acrid smell.
Habitat & distribution: Along roadsides and on freshly gravelled sites; clustered and occasionally in large numbers; frequent.
The fungus is not poisonous, but consumption is not advised because of the danger of confusion with poisonous, white clitocybes. Also, because *L. connatum* was recently discovered to contain lyophyllin, the chemical structure of which is similar to chemical structures which cause gene damage.
Similar species: There are several, mostly grey-capped lyophyllums with white, rather thick, sinuous gills which discolour blue or black in some species. Some entolomas can also bare a resemblance to the white- or grey-capped lyophyllums, but they are distinguished by having pink gills.

56

57

58 *Clitocybe vibecina* ☠

Cap: Umbilicated with down-turned margin, rarely funnel-shaped; when moist, dark grey with brownish-grey centre; translucent at margin, striped and whitish-grey when dry; to 5 cm in diameter.
Gills: Dirty grey; rather thick, a little decurrent. *Spores:* White.
Stem: Grey, white, apex pruinose.
Flesh: Watery grey, with mealy, rancid smell.
Habitat & distribution: In rows and rings on needle litter, usually late in the year; very frequent.
Similar species: Clitocybe ditopus is larger. Its cap is also grey when moist, white when dry, but the ribs are absent. It smells strongly mealy and also grows on needle litter, often with *C. vibecina*.

59 *Collybia dryophila* ☠ Russet Tough-shank

Cap: Convex or flat and expanded; light orange-brown when moist, pale buff when dry, not striped; flesh thin; to 5 cm in diameter.
Gills: White, can be clay-coloured or yellowish when old; thin and crowded, with smooth edge, sinuate. *Spores:* White.
Stem: Same colour as cap; smooth and hollow.
Flesh: Brownish-white, pleasant smell.
Habitat & distribution: Communal, but not clustered, in deciduous and coniferous forests; often from May; frequent.
Similar species: The stem of *Collybia hariolorum* is hairy at the base and smells strongly of decayed cabbage; on leaf litter of beech.

60 *Macrocystidia cucumis* ☠

Cap: Convex to flat; dark red to blackish-brown with lighter rim when moist; very much paler and ochreous when dry; to 5 cm in diameter.
Gills: White, later reddish, quite crowded. *Spores:* Pale ochre.
Stem: Colour as cap, lighter at apex; thin; velvety at base.
Flesh: White; very strong smell of freshly cut cucumbers.
Habitat & distribution: Communal, in large numbers on needle litter, remains of bark or moist soil; rather frequent.

61 *Clitocybe brumalis* ☠ Winter Funnel Cap

Cap: Convex or umbilicate when young, soon rather funnel-shaped; when moist, pale buff, margin weakly translucent and striped, almost white when dry; to 5 cm in diameter.
Gills: Dirty white; crowded, a little decurrent. *Spores:* White.
Stem: Buff to pale brown; striped and soon hollow, with white, felted base.
Flesh: Dirty flesh-brown; with weak mealy smell or odourless.
Habitat & distribution: In deciduous and coniferous woodlands, only in winter; sometimes even under snow.
Similar species: Several similarly coloured species that grow in autumn are difficult to distinguish.

58

left
59

right
60

61

62 *Rickenella fibula* ☠ Orange Moss Agaric

Cap: Convex or umbilicate; orange, ribbed margin; to 1 cm in diameter.
Gills: White, thick, distant, deeply decurrent. *Spores:* White.
Stem: Concolorous with cap; very long.
Habitat & distribution: In coniferous forests among moss, also in meadows and fens; frequent.

63 *Galerina hypnorum* ☠

Cap: Bell-shaped, thin pellicle; light honey-brown and ribbed when moist; yellowish-brown when dry; to 1 cm in diameter.
Gills: Pale rust-brown. *Spores:* Rust-brown.
Stem: Yellowish-brown, with whitish fibres or flocci, apex pruinose.
Habitat & distribution: Coniferous forests among moss; very frequent.

64 *Mycena fagetorum* ☠

Cap: Conical with strong, wart-shaped umbo; dark greyish-brown, with lighter margin, gills make translucent margin striped; 1.5 cm in diameter.
Gills: White or light grey. *Spores:* White.
Stem: Greyish-brown; smooth, hollow, felted at base.
Flesh: Smells mealy.
Habitat & distribution: In large groups and often in clusters, on beech litter; not frequent.

65 *Mycena galopus* ☠ Milk Drop Mycena

Cap: Bell-shaped; light whitish-grey to almost black; moist, ribbed by gills below thin, translucent pellicle; to 1.5 cm diameter.
Gills: White; distant. *Spores:* White.
Stem: Greyish-brown, smooth, long, slender, exuding white milk if damaged.
Habitat & distribution: From June, in coniferous forests, among moss; frequent.

66 *Mycena epipterygia* ☠ Yellow-stemmed Mycena

Cap: Bell-shaped; light grey to greyish-brown; moist, ribbed, with a rubbery, extendible pellicle which can be pulled off; to 2.5 cm in diameter.
Gills: White; with extendible edge which pulls off. *Spores:* White.
Stem: Lemon-yellow; bare and smooth, with rubbery skin.
Habitat & distribution: From September, in clusters in deciduous and coniferous forests, also on stumps; frequent.

67 *Entoloma cetratum* ☠

Cap: Broadly conical to convex, with small umbo; light amber-brown, ribbed almost to centre; 2-3 cm in diameter.
Gills: Salmon-pink; sinuate. *Spores:* Pink.
Stem: Light brownish; longitudinally fibrous and silky; slender.
Habitat & distribution: From May, mostly singly in coniferous forests among moss; rather frequent.

left
62
right
63

left
64
right
65

left
66
right
67

68 ## *Mycena aurantiomarginata* ☠

Cap: Broadly bell-shaped with prominent umbo; light greyish-brown, rather grooved when moist; to 2 cm in diameter.
Gills: Pale greyish-brown, edge bright orange-yellow. *Spores:* White.
Stem: Pale yellow- to greyish-brown; smooth.
Habitat & distribution: In large numbers on needle litter; frequent.

69 ## *Mycena rosella* ☠

Cap: Convex; pale pink, transparent, striped; to 1.5 cm in diameter.
Gills: Pale pink, with red edge. *Spores:* White.
Stem: Pinkish-brown; frequently with white hairs at base.
Habitat & distribution: From end of September, on needle litter; frequent.

70 ## *Mycena pura* ☠ Lilac Mycena

Cap: Bell-shaped, becoming flat, with broad umbo; pinkish-brown, blue-violet or greyish-lilac; when dry white to steel grey, margin striped when moist, up to 5 cm in diameter.
Gills: White or pale pink; deeply sinuate. *Spores:* White.
Stem: Concolorous with the cap or white; felted at the base; hollow.
Flesh: With strong smell of radish.
Habitat & distribution: In deciduous and coniferous forests, from June to November; frequent.
This fungus contains a little muscarin, but is not dangerously poisonous.

71 ## *Mycena pelianthina* ☠

Cap: At first convex to umbonate, soon flat; when moist, dirty violet-grey with striped margin, dirty whitish-grey when dry; to 5 cm in diameter.
Gills: Dirty grey-violet, floccose, black-purplish edge. *Spores:* White.
Stem: Concolorous with cap, longitudinally striped, hollow.
Flesh: With strong smell of radish.
Habitat & distribution: From June in deciduous woodlands, particularly in deep beech leaf litter; rather frequent.
It is likely that this fungus contains muscarin like *M. pura* (70).

72 ## *Omphalina sphagnicola* ☠ ☒

Cap: Deeply funnel-shaped and umbilicate; light brownish-grey to buff, often with small scales, with striped margin; to 2 cm in diameter.
Gills: Dirty-white; distant and deeply decurrent. *Spores:* White.
Stem: Concolorous with cap; smooth.
Habitat & distribution: Only in fens; fairly rare and should be protected.

73 ## *Strobilurus esculentus* ☠

Cap: Convex; brownish-grey, also off-white or black-brown; 1-3 cm in diameter.
Gills: White; crowded, somewhat sinuate. *Spores:* White.
Stem: Brownish-grey with pale apex; a little floccose.
Habitat & distribution: In spring on fallen pine cones; very frequent.

left
68
right
69

left
70
right
71

left
72
right
73

74 *Marasmius torquescens* ☠

Cap: Broadly convex to flat, with weak, broad umbo; when moist buff-yellow and striped, as the gills can be seen through the translucent margin; straw-coloured when dry; to 3 cm in diameter.
Gills: Light buff, sinuate, thick, rather distant. *Spores:* White.
Stem: Yellowish at the apex; towards base increasingly red- to black-brown; tough, hollow, bare and smooth.
Flesh: Buff-yellow, no scent or taste.
Habitat & distribution: Mostly in larger groups in deciduous forests particularly among leaf litter of beech, occasionally on needle litter.
Similar species: Marasmius cohaerens has a red-brown cap and a glossy red-brown stem with a black base and also grows on beech leaf litter.

75 *Micromphale brassicolens* ☠

Cap: Convex to flat, indistinctly umbonate, contorted when old; red-brown and strongly striped when moist, paler when dry; to 4 cm in diameter.
Gills: Dirty off-white, can be reddish grey-brown when old; moderately crowded. *Spores:* White.
Stem: Red-brown at apex, increasingly black towards base, with a slight bloom, often flattened, hollow.
Flesh: With strong smell of decaying cabbage.
Habitat & distribution: In clusters or singly in great numbers on beech leaf litter, also on needle litter; fairly rare.

76 *Marasmius scorodonius* ☺

Cap: Bell-shaped, soon convex and usually contorted; ochre-brown and striped at margin; pale buff when dry; thin pellicle; 1-2 cm in diameter.
Gills: Dirty buff, thick, distant. *Spores:* White.
Stem: Light red-brown, tough, bare and smooth.
Flesh: With strong smell of garlic, used as a spice.
Habitat & distribution: In great numbers on needle litter; frequent.

77 *Marasmius androsaceus* ☠

Horsehair toadstool

Cap: Convex, usually furrowed and contorted; light buff to brownish; thin pellicle; to 1 cm in diameter.
Gills: Dirty buff, thick, distant, connected ring-like at stem.
Stem: Dark black-brown, thin, tough, resembling horse hair.
Flesh: Without smell of garlic.
Habitat & distribution: In great masses on pine needle litter after rain.

78 *Micromphale perforans* ☠

Cap: Convex, irregularly contorted; pale buff to flesh-coloured; thin-skinned; to 1.5 cm in diameter.
Gills: Off-white; thick and distant. *Spores:* White.
Stem: Black, with white apex, tough.
Flesh: With unpleasant, garlic-like smell.
Habitat & distribution: On needle litter, mostly after rain; frequent.

left
74
right
75

76

left
77
right
78

79 *Collybia acervata* ☠

Cap: Domed convex; when moist rust-brown, pellicle translucent and gills appear as stripes; dirty flesh-brown when dry; to 5 cm in diameter.
Gills: Off-white to pale cream; very crowded, sinuate. *Spores:* White.
Stem: Orange- to red-brown; bare, glossy, base felted, often flattened.
Flesh: Smelling weakly of decaying cabbage.
Habitat & distribution: In coniferous forests in clusters on roots and around stumps, mostly at higher altitudes; fairly rare.

80 *Flammulina velutipes* ☺ Velvet Shank

Cap: At first convex with rather striped margin, soon flat; lovely chestnut-brown; weakly sticky; mostly 2-5 cm in diameter.
Gills: White, then pale yellow; mostly distant. *Spores:* White.
Stem: At the apex light, towards the base red- to black-brown and minutely velvety; no ring.
Flesh: Yellowish; mild taste and pleasant smell.
Habitat & distribution: In mild winters, occasionally appears in October in clusters on deciduous wood, mainly on beech, rarely on coniferous wood.
Use: The caps can provide tasty winter meals if plentiful enough. This fungus is easily cultivated, but as harvests are small it has no economic importance as a crop.
Similar species: Also during winter but on conifer wood appears *Hypholoma capnoides* (182) which has a more orange-yellow cap. Velvet shank can also be confused with the very poisonous *Galerina marginata* (180) and with other brown-capped, clustering fungal species which do not, however, grow in winter.

81 *Xeromphalina campanella* ☠

Cap: Bell-shaped, later somewhat umbilicated at centre; light rust-brown with striped margin, growing paler; to 2 cm in diameter.
Gills: White to cream; thick, distant, decurrent and transversely connected. *Spores:* White.
Stem: Dark rust-brown, often somewhat squashed, with yellow and often broadening apex.
Habitat & distribution: Throughout the year, mainly in spring and autumn on stumps of conifers, mostly in large number.
Similar species: Several galerinas are similar in shape and colour of the cap, their stem is never black-brown, however, but light brown.

82 *Collybia confluens* ☠ Clustered Tough Shank

Cap: First conical, then bell-shaped or expanded; buff and weakly striped when moist, paler when dry; to 3 cm in diameter.
Gills: Dirty white; narrow and very crowded. *Spores:* White.
Stem: Pale buff; minutely felted, hairy at base, hollow; apex can be detached from flesh of cap.
Habitat & distribution: In clusters on leaf and needle litter; often in large groups and in fairy rings.

79

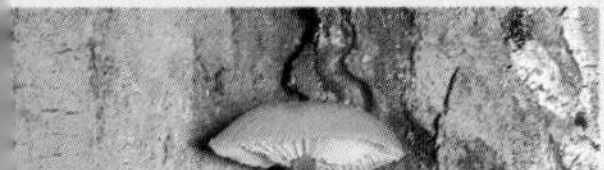

left
80
right
81

82

83 *Marasmius oreades* ☺ Fairy Ring Champignon

Cap: Convex, margin a little striped when moist; pale buff or light red-brown; to 5 cm in diameter.
Gills: Pale buff; thick and rather distant, deeply sinuate. *Spores:* White.
Stem: Pale yellowish-buff; with minutely floccose layer.
Flesh: Yellowish-white; mild taste; smelling of fresh saw dust.
Habitat & distribution: Mostly in large groups or fairy rings in meadows and on forest fringes among grass; frequent.

84 *Rhodocybe nitellina* ☠

Cap: Convex to flat or somewhat funnel-shaped; orange to light red-brown, striped when moist as the gills can be seen through the translucent pellicle; mostly 2-4 cm in diameter.
Gills: First white, later cream-orange; crowded. *Spores:* Pale pink.
Stem: Concolorous with cap, white pruinose at apex; hollow when old.
Flesh: With strong mealy smell.
Habitat & distribution: In deciduous and coniferous woodland, mostly communally at waysides; not rare.

85 *Collybia butyracea* ☠ Greasy Tough-shank

Cap: Hemispherical when young, soon convex, rarely flat; lovely red-brown and glossy when moist, paler when dry; mostly 4-6 cm in diameter.
Gills: White, no rust-coloured spots, crowded, with coarsely notched edge, sinuate. *Spores:* White.
Stem: Pale red-brown, longitudinally striped, bare; with a swollen base, hollow when old.
Flesh: White, mild taste, with pleasant smell of butter.
Habitat & distribution: Communally in coniferous and deciduous forests; often in fairy rings; frequent.
Similar species: Collybia distorta in coniferous forests has an irregularly distorted cap, a strongly twisted thinner stem and coarsely denticulate gills with many rust spots when old.

86 *Collybia butyracea var. asema* ☠

Cap: In form and size as *C. butyracea* (85), but dark grey-brown, becoming paler whitish-grey when dry.
Stem: Light grey-brown; otherwise as *C. butyracea.*
Gills / Flesh / Habitat & distribution: As *C. butyracea.*

87 *Collybia peronata* ☠

Cap: First convex, soon flat; pale yellow reddish-brown, turning a little lighter when dry; flesh thin, leathery; to 5 cm in diameter.
Gills: Light yellow reddish-brown; very thick, distant. *Spores:* White.
Stem: Pale yellowish-brown; lower half hairy and felted.
Flesh: Tough, very hot, burning on the tongue.
Habitat & distribution: Usually in large numbers or in clusters on moist leaf litter, but also on needle litter; frequent.

left
83
right
84

85

left
86
right
87

88 *Pluteus plautus* ☠ ☒

Cap: Bell-shaped to flat; dark brown and minutely velvety when young, later scaly; 2-4 cm in diameter.
Gills: Flesh-pink, edge often brownish when old. *Spores:* Pink.
Stem: Dark brown; evenly thick, with minute scales.
Habitat & distribution: Mostly singly on conifer wood; fairly rare, and should not be picked.

89 *Pseudoclitocybe cyathiformis* ☠

Cap: Deeply umbilicate with initially inrolled margin which often becomes contorted later; dark greyish-brown, grey when dry; to 6 cm in diameter.
Gills: Greyish-brown, sometimes forked, decurrent. *Spores:* White.
Stem: Greyish-brown, white and felted at base.
Habitat & distribution: In late autumn in meadows and coniferous forests with grassy floors; very frequent.

90 *Entoloma nidorosum* ☠

Cap: Convex or depressed, even umblilicate; greyish-brown and a little grooved when moist, whitish-grey and glossy when dry; 3-6 cm in diameter.
Gills: White, then salmon-pink, rather thick, distant. *Spores:* Pink.
Stem: Whitish-grey; rather long and slender.
Flesh: Whitish; with strong nitric smell, reminiscent of ammonia.
Habitat & distribution: In deciduous woodland; often in fairy rings; rather frequent. Weakly poisonous: can cause gastric problems.

91 *Entoloma nitidum* ☠

Cap: Broad, bell-shaped, frequently with blunt umbo; dark steel blue; to 5 cm in diameter.
Gills: Dirty salmon-pink; thick, distant. *Spores:* Pink.
Stem: Concolorous with cap, striped over a white felted base.
Habitat & distribution: Singly or in groups in moist coniferous mountain forests; rare at lower altitudes.

92 *Clitopilus prunulus* ☠

Cap: Hemispherical when young, later convex to flat; dirty white, with thick flesh; 3-12 cm in diameter.
Gills: At first light cream-pink, later dirty brownish; moderately crowded, deeply decurrent. *Spores:* Pink.
Stem: Dirty white; fibrous, felted base. *Flesh:* White; with mealy smell.
Habitat & distribution: In deciduous and coniferous forests; frequent.
Similar species: Beware confusion with poisonous *Clitocybe dealbata* (56).

93 *Lyophyllum fumosum* ☺

Cap: Convex, later irregularly contorted; dark greyish-brown, fibrous and striped; mostly 4-6 cm in diameter.
Gills: White, later light grey, sinuate. *Spores:* White.
Stem: Whitish grey, evenly thick. *Flesh:* Smell of flour, mild taste.
Habitat & distribution: In ense clusters on grassland, rare in woodland.

left
88
right
89

left
90
right
91

left
92
right
93

94 *Marasmius alliaceus* ☠ **Garlic Mushroom**

Cap: Broad, convex, a little wrinkly; pale buff, often blotchy, almost white when dry; to 4 cm in diameter.
Gills: Dirty whitish; narrow and distant. *Spores:* White.
Stem: Black-brown with light apex; very long and slender, stiff, hollow, minutely pruinose, rooting in soil.
Flesh: With strong smell of garlic.
Habitat & distribution: Mostly on fallen branches of deciduous trees more rarely on leaf or needle litter; from May; frequent.

95 *Marasmius rotula* ☠ **Little Wheel Toadstool**

Cap: Convex with umbilicate centre, radial grooves dissect expanded margin; white, membranous; to 1 cm in diameter.
Gills: White; thick and distant, fusing in ring around stem. *Spores:* White.
Stem: Black-brown with light apex; thin, like horse hair.
Habitat & distribution: Clusters on twigs of deciduous wood; frequent.

96 *Marasmiellus ramealis* ☠

Cap: Convex, later mostly flat; pale rust-brown; to 1 cm in diameter.
Gills: White; distant. *Spores:* White.
Stem: White, pruinose, turning brownish with age, thin.
Habitat & distribution: Communal, but not in clusters, on twigs of deciduous wood.

97 *Nyctalis parasitica* ☠

Cap: First conical, later broadly bell-shaped; margin with fibrous veil; whitish-grey; thin flesh; to 1.5 cm in diameter.
Gills: Whitish-grey, later blackening and dissolving, thick, distant.
Spores: White.
Stem: Whitish-grey; slender, a little floccose.
Flesh: Whitish-grey; with mealy smell.
Habitat & distribution: Only on decaying russulas and lactarias; fairly rare.

98 *Mycena haematopus* ☠ **Bleeding Mycena**

Cap: Bell-shaped with tufts on the margin; dark purple-brown, a little striped when moist, paling with age; to 2 cm in diameter.
Gills: White, with serrate edge. *Spores:* White.
Stem: Pale purplish-brown, purple-red towards base; exudes blackish-red staining milk sap when damaged; somewhat pruinose.
Habitat & distribution: In clusters on deciduous wood and on stumps; not rare.

99 *Micromphale foetidum* ☠

Cap: Convex, then flat, striped margin; dirty brownish-red; 2 cm in diameter.
Gills: Reddish-grey; thick, a little distant. *Spores:* White.
Stem: Blackish-brown; minutely pruinose.
Flesh: Strong smell of decaying cabbage.
Habitat & distribution: On dead deciduous wood, mostly Hazel branches.

left **94**
right **95**

left **96**
right **97**

left **98**
right **99**

100 *Hygrocybe coccineocrenata* ☠ ☒

Cap: Convex, soon flat and frequently with a depressed centre; bright scarlet-red, particularly in the centre, with minute, darker scales; margin a little crenate; 1-3 cm in diameter.
Gills: White, becoming light yellow; thick and decurrent. *Spores:* White.
Stem: Orange- to scarlet-red; rather long and slender.
Flesh: Reddish; very brittle, mild taste.
Habitat & distribution: In groups in fens or moist meadows on grass.

101 *Hygrocybe nigrescens* ☠

Cap: Acutely conical, later expanded and with prominent umbo; lemon-yellow to orange-red, turning black slowly; to 4 cm in diameter.
Gills: White, then pale yellowish, blackish-grey when old; thick, distant.
Spores: White.
Stem: White to orange, turning black from the base; very fragile.
Flesh: Yellowish-white; without scent, mild taste.
Habitat & distribution: On lawns and pastures; considered poisonous.

102 *Hygrocybe psittacina* ☠ Parrot Toadstool

Cap: First conical, soon flat or umbonate; grass-green, becoming lemon- or orange-yellow, lilac or orange-brown; to 4 cm in diameter.
Gills: Greenish, orange and yellowish; thick, distant. *Spores:* White.
Stem: Pale greenish, towards base also yellow or orange, sticky.
Flesh: Very brittle, no scent, mild taste.
Habitat & distribution: On poor meadows and pastures; rare.

103 *Hygrophorus eburneus* ☠ Ivory Slime Cap

Cap: Convex when young, flat when old; white and very slimy; with long inrolled and rather downy, crenate margin; to 6 cm in diameter.
Gills: White, thick, distant, decurrent when old. *Spores:* White.
Stem: White; long and slender, base acuminate, rooting deeply in ground, apex somewhat white, floccose, very slimy towards base.
Flesh: White; mild taste, with unpleasant smell.
Habitat & distribution: Mostly in groups in deep beech leaf litter; frequent.
Similar species: H. discoxanthus, distinguished by orange-brown surface of cap and gills when older.

104 *Hygrophorus chrysodon* ☠ Yellow Downy Hygrophorus

Cap: Convex, later flat or with blunt umbo; very slimy; pure white with lemon yellow tufts particularly at rim; to 6 cm in diameter.
Gills: White; thick and distant. *Spores:* White.
Stem: White; with yellow tufts at least at apex.
Flesh: White; mild taste, without scent.
Habitat & distribution: In groups under spruce; more rarely also in deciduous woodland; mostly at higher altitudes.

left
100
right
101

102

left
103
right
104

105 *Hygrophorus pudorinus* ☠

Cap: Convex, soon flat, slippery; bright orange, glossy when dry and often turning yellow; long inrolled margin, crenate and minutely felted; up to 15 cm in diameter.
Gills: Pale cream-pink; thick, distant, adnate or slightly decurrent.
Spores: White.
Stem: First white or orange-pink, later turning beautifully yellow from the base; minutely floccose and rather sticky.
Flesh: Orange, yellow within the stem base; tastes of turpentine.
Habitat & distribution: Only below silver fir on chalk, often in mixed beech woodland.
Similar species: Hygrophorus poetarum is more orange-red; without yellow stem, no taste of turpentine. Mainly in beech woods.

106 *Hygrophorus discoideus* ☠

Cap: Bell-shaped, soon flat with broad and very flat umbo; dark red-brown at the centre, at margin light orange- or reddish-brown; very slimy when moist; to 6 cm in diameter.
Gills: Light cream; thick, distant, decurrent when old. *Spores:* White.
Stem: Cream-white; sticky, at apex with light tufts.
Flesh: Cream; mild taste, no scent.
Habitat & distribution: From September in coniferous forests, particularly on needle litter; very communal.
Similar species: Hygrophorus leucophaeus has a paler cap with an almost white margin; only slightly slippery; in deciduous woodland.

107 *Hygrophorus agathosmus* ☠

Cap: Convex when young, later flat or somewhat funnel-shaped; light grey; very slimy when young, later mostly dry, somewhat glossy and minutely grainy; up to 6 cm in diameter.
Gills: White; thick and distant, decurrent. *Spores:* White.
Stem: White, with dirty-white or yellowish tufts; evenly thick, dry.
Flesh: White; with strong sweetish scent of bitter almonds.
Habitat & distribution: Predominantly among grass along waysides; in coniferous forests, frequent.

108 *Hygrophorus erubescens* ☠

Cap: Convex, soon flat and usually irregularly contorted; slippery; white skin with wine- to purplish-red blotches, sometimes almost completely white or evenly purple; to 10 cm in diameter.
Gills: First white, soon with wine-red blotches; thick, somewhat distant, decurrent when old. *Spores:* White.
Stem: White, with wine-red tufts.
Flesh: White, turning slowly yellow when bruised; usually has a weakly bitter taste, no scent.
Habitat & distribution: Sometimes in great masses, predominantly in coniferous forests; not frequent.

105

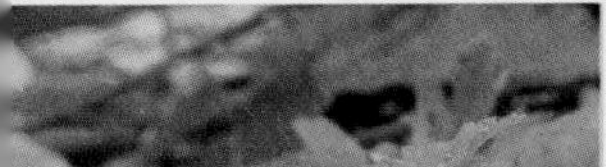

left
106
right
107

108

109 *Hygrophorus marzuolus* ☺☒

Cap: Convex, soon spreading; whitish-grey to grey-black; slightly slippery, soon dry and somewhat striped; to 7 cm in diameter.
Gills: At first pure white, turning grey when old; thick, distant and moderately decurrent. *Spores:* White.
Stem: First white, later light grey; evenly thick, rather short, firm.
Flesh: White; mild taste, no scent.
Habitat & distribution: From March to May, mostly communally in coniferous forests at higher altitudes; fairly rare.
Similar species: There are several other grey-capped hygrophoruses which are mostly very slimy and do not grow in spring.

110 *Hygrophorus olivaceoalbus* ☠

Cap: Initially convex, then expanded with inrolled margin and usually with small umbo; can be funnel-shaped when old; dirty olive-grey; very slimy; lighter and somewhat glossy when dry; to 6 cm in diameter.
Gills: White; thick and distant, short decurrent. *Spores:* White.
Stem: Apex white and somewhat floccose with snake pattern starting from below olive-grey slime cover; long.
Flesh: White; without scent, mild taste.
Habitat & distribution: In moist coniferous forests, among moss, mostly frequent.
Similar species: Hygrophorus dichrous is larger, has a thicker stem and grows in deciduous forests.

111 *Gomphidius roseus* ☠

Cap: Convex, later flat; beautifully pink, slippery; mostly 2-4 cm in diameter.
Gills: Thick, distant, decurrent; first white, turning grey when old due to ripe spores. *Spores:* Olive-black.
Stem: Pure white, turning somewhat yellow towards the base; attenuate; with a translucent slime layer that can be wiped off and disappears later.
Flesh: White, yellow within base; soft, without scent, mild taste.
Habitat & distribution: Only under pines, mostly together with *Suillus bovinus* (32); not frequent.

112 *Gomphidius glutinosus* ☺

Cap: Initially convex, later flat; light greyish-brown when young, a blotchy black later; covered by a thick, translucent layer of slime that can be pulled off; in the young fungus this extends across the gills to the base of the stem; up to 10 cm in diameter.
Gills: First pure white, later increasingly grey due to the spores ripening; thick, distant, decurrent. *Spores:* Olive-black.
Stem: At first white, a yellow discolouration starts at base, becoming blotchy when old; evenly thick; top margin of slime cover black from spores.
Flesh: White, reddening a little with age; rather soft; no scent, mild taste.
Habitat & distribution: Under conifers, mostly in small groups; frequent.

109

left
110
right
111

112

113 *Clitocybe nebularis* ☺ Clouded Clitocybe

Cap: At first convex with inrolled margin, later flat, but never funnel-shaped; light smoky grey to greyish-brown; minutely pruinose and rim often wavily contorted when old; fleshy; to 15 cm in diameter.
Gills: White or light cream; very crowded, decurrent; easily detachable from flesh of cap. *Spores:* White.
Stem: White, somewhat fibrous and striped; short, thick, with coarsely club-shaped and often white felted base; compresses needle litter.
Flesh: White; with strongly acrid, mealy and rancid smell.
Habitat & distribution: From September in rows and fairy rings, in deciduous and coniferous forests; frequent.
This fungus is edible, but has a strong, characteristic taste. It can occasionally cause gastric problems, particularly when young fruitbodies have been consumed. The clouded clitocybe is peculiar in its genus as it never has a funnel-shaped cap. The parasitic *Volvariella surrecta* grows on the caps of decaying *C. nebularis*. It is very small, white-capped, has pink gills and a membranous sheath at its base.
Similar species: Clitocybe alexandri has deeper yellow gills and its cap becomes depressed when old; it too forms fairy rings. Beware confusing *C. nebularis* with the poisonous *Entoloma sinuatum* (114).

114 *Entoloma sinuatum* ☠ ☒

Cap: Convex when young, soon flat, usually with broad, blunt umbo; light silver-grey, becoming pale when dry, occasionally ivory-white; minutely scaly and often rather striped; to 20 cm in diameter.
Gills: Cream-yellow, soon salmon-pink; rather crowded, sinuate, not decurrent; cannot be detached from flesh of cap. *Spores:* Pink.
Stem: Whitish-grey and rather glossy; long and slender, base occasionally slightly club-shaped.
Flesh: White; distinctly mealy smell, pleasant taste.
Habitat & distribution: In rows and fairy rings, in deciduous forests, often together with the extremely similar clouded clitocybe. Shortly after consumption the fungus causes violent vomiting and diarrhoea which continues for several days.
Similar species: Lepista irina (124) which also grows in fairy rings; *L.irina* has permanently cream-white gills and smells powerfully sweet. The genus *Entoloma* contains numerous fungi of variable colour and size; but most have hexagonal, pink spores. When the spores are ripe, the initially white or grey gills become light salmon-pink to dirty pinkish-brown in all species. Many species grow on meadows, many appearing as early as the spring. The identification of individual entolomas can in many cases only be achieved with a microscope.

113

114

115 *Clitocybe clavipes* ☠ Club-Footed Clitocybe

Cap: Hemispherical when young, soon broadly convex to flat or umbonate; light brownish-grey and usually soggy, paler when dry; fleshy; to 6 cm in diameter.
Gills: Cream-white; distant, deeply decurrent. *Spores:* White.
Stem: Concolorous with cap; evenly swollen; coarsely club-shaped base.
Flesh: White; extremely soggy, very brittle; rancid, mealy smell.
Habitat & distribution: Communally and often in fairy rings, in moist, mossy conifer forests; frequent.
The fungus is not considered poisonous, but can be when consumed with alcohol.
Similar species: Collybia butyracea (86) is smaller, its gills are white, crowded and sinuate. The cap of *Clitopilus prunulus* (92) is similar in shape, but its stem is not club-shaped and its gills soon assume a cream-pink colour. Its very much firmer flesh smells mealy. Young *Clitocybe entoloma* can also be confused with *C. clavipes. C. entoloma* has firmer flesh with an acrid smell and more crowded gills which can be detached from the flesh of the cap.

116 *Clitocybe odora* ☠ Blue-green Clitocybe

Cap: Convex when young, later flat or irregularly contorted, but only rarely funnel-shaped; colour varies from dirty blue-green to pale blue-grey or green-grey; fleshy; to 10 cm in diameter.
Gills: Whitish-grey; crowded, adnate, can become decurrent when old.
Spores: White.
Stem: White to pale grey-green; evenly thick or weakly club-shaped; somewhat fibrous, white felted at base.
Flesh: White; mild taste; smells of aniseed.
Habitat & distribution: In deciduous and coniferous forests, mostly in groups or fairy rings; quite frequent.

117 *Clitocybe geotropa* ☺

Cap: From the start funnel-shaped with long inrolled margin, almost always with small umbo; pale buff when young, paling with age; silky and pruinose when young; fleshy; to 25 cm in diameter.
Gills: First white, later pale buff; thin and rather crowded, decurrent.
Spores: White.
Stem: Buff; long and slender, occasionally somewhat widened at base. a little fibrous longitudinally; growing more quickly than the cap.
Flesh: Cream-white, mild taste; with sweet, mealy smell.
Habitat & distribution: In deciduous and coniferous forests, prefers moist areas, mostly in fairy rings; not rare.

115

116

117

118 *Calocybe gambosa* ☺ St George's Mushroom

Cap: Hemispherical when young, later convex to flat; at first cream-white, can be ochreous when old; minutely pruinose; to 10 cm in diameter.
Gills: White, crowded, sinuate. *Spores:* White.
Stem: Cream-white; evenly thick and with fibrous scales.
Flesh: White; very mealy smell, mild taste.
Habitat & distribution: May to June on meadows, at forest fringes and in light, deciduous forests; mostly in fairy rings, not rare.
Use: In this season when there are few mushrooms, *C.gambosa* can be recommended as a mushroom vegetable in spite of its disturbing, mealy smell; not for drying.
Similar species: There is a danger of confusing it with the inedible or weakly poisonous hebelomas (p. 118) and with the very poisonous *Inocybe erubescens* (217) which grows during the same season in similar habitats.

119 *Clitocybe gibba* ☠

Cap: Usually funnel-shaped from the start with long inrolled, lighter rim which is often wavily contorted when old; sometimes with small umbo; light ochre-brown when moist, pale buff when dry; to 8 cm in diameter.
Gills: Cream-white; crowded, deeply decurrent. *Spores:* White.
Stem: Whitish when young, later ochre-brown; rather long and slender.
Flesh: Whitish; weak scent, occasionally reminiscent of bitter almonds.
Habitat & distribution: From June in deciduous and coniferous forests; very frequent.

120 *Lepista gilva* ☠

Cap: Flat when young, with long inrolled and somewhat felted margin, soon slightly funnel-shaped; light yellowish-ochre when moist and with water stains particularly at the rim, pale yellowish when dry; to 8 cm in diameter.
Gills: White when young, soon cream-yellow; thin, crowded and deeply decurrent. *Spores:* White.
Stem: Ochre-yellow, like the cap; evenly thick.
Habitat & distribution: Communally and often in fairy rings; in deciduous and coniferous forests; frequent.
Similar species: The cap of *Lepista flaccida* is red-brown and not blotchy when moist, when dry, the cap pales to light reddish-yellow with orange-brown gills. It grows from September in deciduous and coniferous woodlands.

121 *Calocybe onychina* ☠

Cap: Convex or bell-shaped when young, later flat to slightly funnel-shaped, often irregularly contorted; first purplish-brown, later paler and yellowish; to 5 cm in diameter.
Gills: Bright golden yellow; thin, crowded, sinuate. *Spores:* White.
Stem: Pale brownish, overcast with purplish bloom, white-felted at base.
Flesh: Yellowish-white, slightly bitter taste, no scent.
Habitat & distribution: Mostly in groups in coniferous highland forests; rare.

118

left
119
right
120

121

122 *Lepista nuda* ☺ **Wood Blewit**

Cap: First convex, later flat, often a little contorted, dark lilac when young, later pink-lilac or violet-brown; bare, smooth; to 12 cm in diameter.
Gills: Pale lilac; crowded, sinuate. *Spores:* Cream-pink.
Stem: Lilac; rather short, weakly bulbous base, somewhat fibrous.
Flesh: Deep lilac, with sweet smell and mild taste.
Habitat & distribution: In rows and rings, in deciduous and coniferous forests; very frequent.
Similar species: Lepista sordida is smaller and dirty lilac-brown, but it has the same sweet smell. It often grows in clusters and prefers waysides. The violet-capped cortinarias (see p. 125), among which inedible species are found, are similar in colouration. When looked at very carefully they can be distinguished by the veil which extends between margin and stem, and later forms a fibrous ring-zone, stained rust-brown by spores. The gills of cortinarias, lilac or grey at first, are mostly rust-brown when old.

123 *Lepista personata* ☺

Cap: In shape resembling the wood blewit (122) entirely, but is pale lilac and mostly whitish-grey.
Gills: As wood blewit (122), but dirty cream-coloured. *Spores:* Cream-pink.
Stem: As wood blewit; deeply blue-violet when young.
Flesh: Deep lilac in stem; whitish-grey in the cap.
Habitat & distribution: In October and November, in meadows and at waysides, mostly in rows and rings.
Similar species: Lepista glaucocana is pale pink-lilac throughout, but otherwise shares all the characteristics of *Lepista nuda* (122) and *L. personata* (123). It also grows in fairy rings, mainly in mountain forests and is not rare. *L. panaeola* grows on dry meadows and has the same shape but is distinguished by its even grey-brown colouration and by the total absence of lilac hues.

124 *Lepista irina* ☠

Cap: Convex when young, later irregularly arched, with long inrolled, pruinose and occasionally notched margin; pale cream-white; to 8 cm in diameter.
Gills: Pale cream when young, later dirty flesh-coloured; crowded, sinuate. *Spores:* Cream.
Stem: Cream; rather long, evenly thick, a little fibrous.
Flesh: Cream; strong sweet smell of iris or root of violet.
Habitat & distribution: In deciduous or coniferous forests, growing almost always in rows or circles; frequent in some areas.
Similar species: Calocybe gambosa (118) is externally similar, but it grows in spring and smells distinctly mealy. *L. irina* could also be confused with the poisonous *Entoloma sinuatum* (114).

122

123

124

125 *Tricholoma aurantium* ☠

Cap: Convex when young, later flat; bright orange-brown; rather granular and very slippery when moist; fleshy; to 10 cm in diameter.
Gills: White, later brown and blotchy, crowded, sinuate. *Spores:* White.
Stem: Bright orange, concolorous with cap, with sharply distinguished white apex; granular.
Flesh: White; bitter, with strong smell of cucumbers or fresh flour.
Habitat & distribution: Under spruce, in forest grassland, mostly in fairy rings; not frequent.

126 *Tricholoma ustale* ☠ Burnt Tricholoma

Cap: Bell-shaped when young, soon expanded, with blunt umbo and long, inrolled margin; first dark red-brown and very slippery, drying up and becoming black-brown when old; to 8 cm in diameter.
Gills: First white, soon blotchy red-brown, crowded, sinuate. *Spores:* White.
Stem: Light red-brown and usually minutely scaly.
Flesh: White; bitter taste, no scent; can cause gastric problems if eaten.
Habitat & distribution: In deciduous and coniferous forests; mostly in large number; sometimes in clusters.
Similar species: It is extremely difficult to distinguish between the several types of brown-capped tricholomas. Because some are poisonous it is not wise to consume any brown-capped tricholomas.

127 *Tricholoma vaccinum* ☠

Cap: First bell-shaped, later convex to flat, broad umbo; red-brown at apex, diffused into woolly scales towards margin; to 9 cm diameter.
Gills: Cream-white, soon blotchy red-brown, sinuate. *Spores:* White.
Stem: Pale red-brown, slender.
Flesh: White, reddening somewhat; bitter taste.
Habitat & distribution: From September in deciduous and coniferous forests, at waysides, among grass; frequent mainly at higher altitudes.
Similar species: Tricholoma imbricatum grows under pines; it has coarse scales at the margin; but where the margin tears, the light flesh of the cap is revealed. Inocybes can also look similar (p. 120), but their gills discolour to earthy grey, not red-brown.

128 *Tricholomopsis rutilans* ☠

Plums-and-Custard

Cap: Convex; at first densely covered with purple felty scales which partly disappear in time to reveal yellow skin below; mostly 6-8 cm, rarely to 20 cm in diameter.
Gills: Light golden yellow; thin, crowded, sinuate. *Spores:* White.
Stem: Yellowish-white skin with purple-red scales on top which disappear later; evenly thick.
Flesh: Yellowish-white; without scent, mild taste.
Habitat & distribution: Only on wood of conifers, mostly on stumps or by their side; frequent.

125

left
126
right
127

128

129 *Tricholoma portentosum* ☺

Dingy Tricholoma

Cap: Hemispherical when young, soon convex to flat; dark greyish-black, rarely also with yellow, green or blueish hues; mostly fibrous and striped, somewhat sticky; to 10 cm in diameter.
Gills: First white, later yellowing; crowded, sinuate. *Spores:* White.
Stem: White, sometimes yellowing when old; a little fibrous.
Flesh: White; with a faint mealy smell.
Habitat: From September, in groups in conifer forests; locally frequent.
Use: Excellent taste, for all culinary purposes.
Similar species: Danger of confusing *T. portentosum* with several similar, slightly poisonous tricholomas; it is important to note the yellow gills.

130 *Tricholoma terreum* ☺

Grey Tricholoma

Cap: Bell-shaped when young, soon conical to flat, often indistinctly umbonate; light grey to black; with minute woolly scales; to 8 cm in diameter.
Gills: Whitish-grey, greying with age; fairly crowded, sinuate, with crenate edges. *Spores:* White.
Stem: Whitish-grey; smooth or with grey woolly fibres; apex pruinose.
Flesh: Whitish-grey, mild taste, weak mealy smell.
Habitat & distribution: In deciduous and coniferous forests; frequent.
Similar species: Danger of confusion with the poisonous *Tricholoma pardalotum* and other weakly poisonous, grey-capped tricholomas.

131 *Tricholoma saponaceum* ☠

Soap-scented Tricholoma

Cap: Convex when young, later flat; colour very variable, mostly whitish-grey to dark greyish-black, but also with olive-green or reddish hues; smooth or scaly; to 12 cm in diameter.
Gills: White, also greenish-grey or reddish, slowly reddening when bruised; thick and distant, sinuate. *Spores:* White.
Stem: Mostly white, with small grey scales; often long; deeply rooted.
Flesh: White when young, turning reddish later; with a smell of soap suds which enables immediate recognition of this otherwise most variable fungus which can cause gastric problems when consumed.
Habitat & distribution: In groups; from September in deciduous and coniferous forests; frequent.

132 *Tricholoma pardalotum* ☠

Cap: Convex when young, soon splitting into woolly scales, later flat or irregularly contorted; at first whitish-grey occasionally assuming brownish or lilac hues when old; to 12 cm in diameter.
Gills: Dirty white or yellowish; thick, distant, sinuate. *Spores:* White.
Stem: White and somewhat fibrous; strong, slightly club-shaped and with water droplets at apex when young.
Flesh: White; mealy smell, mild taste.
Habitat: Mostly communally; deciduous and coniferous forests; frequent. This tasty fungus causes gastric problems that can last for several days.

129

left
130
right
131

132

133 *Tricholoma sulphureum* ☠

Sulphur Knight-Cap

Cap: Almost hemispherical when young, later convex or irregularly funnel-shaped and contorted; initially light sulphur-yellow with reddish-brown centre, greyish-yellow or dirty brown when old; to 7 cm in diameter.
Gills: Bright sulphur-yellow; thick and very distant, deeply sinuate.
Spores: White.
Stem: Light sulphur-yellow; evenly thick or obese, fibrous.
Flesh: Yellow; with strong, unpleasant smell of coal gas; causes gastric problems if consumed.
Habitat & distribution: In deciduous and coniferous woods, mainly along waysides; frequent.
Similar species: Only a beautifully purple-brown cap distinguishes *Tricholoma buffonium* which grows predominantly in coniferous forests. The cap of *Tricholoma inamoenum* is a little smaller and light ochre, its stem is white and has scaly fibres; it grows in coniferous forests and also smells unpleasantly of coal gas.

134 *Tricholoma equestre* ☺☒

Cap: Convex when young, later flat; dirty olive-brown at apex, a lighter greenish-yellow towards margin; very slippery, sand and needle litter tend to stick to it.
Gills: Sulphur-yellow; thin and crowded, sinuate. *Spores:* White.
Stem: Light sulphur-yellow; evenly thick or a little tuberous at base, positioned deeply in soil.
Flesh: Bright lemon-yellow; mild taste, smelling very mealy.
Habitat & distribution: Mostly in coniferous forests, mainly under pines on sandy soil; rare and so should be protected.
Similar species: Tricholoma furcatum frequently grows with *T. equestre*; it is also edible, looks similar, but has white gills.
The cap of *T. sejunctum* has a browner apex; its gills are white at first and discolour to yellow when old. Mistaking it for *T.equestre* could be unpleasant as it tastes bitter and can cause gastric complaints. (Compare fungi with yellow gills on p. 131 and p. 133, among which some species are suspected of being poisonous.)

135 *Tricholoma viridilutescens* ☠

Cap: Convex to flat; often contorted and umbonate; mostly yellowish-green, with black-green apex, but also pure green to olive; often similar in colour to *Amanita phalloides* (146); to 6 cm in diameter.
Gills: First white, later discolouring yellow from the margin, with noticeably coarse serrate edge. *Spores:* White.
Stem: First white, later discolouring yellow; evenly thick.
Flesh: White, turning yellow; mild taste, no mealy smell.
Habitat & distribution: Predominantly in coniferous forests, particularly in the Alps and in northern Europe; rare.

133

134

135

136 *Xerula melanotricha* ☠

Cap: In shape and colour similar to *Xeryla radicata* (137), but dry and velvety dark brown; to 9 cm in diameter.
Gills: White; thick and distant. *Spores:* White.
Stem: Evenly dark brown, velvety; long, rooting very deeply.
Habitat & distribution: Under silver firs; rare.

137 *Xerula radicata* ☠

Cap: First conical, soon flat expanded, with broad umbo; light reddish to yellowish-brown; wrinkly, very slimy; flesh thin; to 8 cm diameter.
Gills: White; thick, distant, sinuate. *Spores:* White.
Stem: Pale brownish, often with stripes; rooting very deeply; tough.
Habitat & distribution: Singly in the beech wood, occasionally on stumps.

138 *Melanoleuca melaleuca* ☠

Changeable Melanoleuca

Cap: Convex when young, soon flat or somewhat funnel-shaped; dark brown-grey; smooth and bare; to 10 cm in diameter.
Gills: White; narrow and very crowded, sinuate. *Spores:* White.
Stem: Lighter brown-grey; very short, base often slightly club-shaped.
Flesh: White; mild taste and without scent.
Habitat & distribution: From May communally in coniferous forests, among grass or along waysides; frequent.
Similar species: Even specialists have difficulties in distinguishing the numerous species of *Melanoleuca* with white to black-brown caps.

139 *Megacollybia platyphylla* ☠

Cap: At first convex, soon flat; light brownish-grey and usually with stripes; dry; up to over 10 cm in diameter.
Gills: White; thick, very broad, distant, deeply sinuate. *Spores:* White.
Stem: Light grey-brown, slightly striped longitudinally; cylindrical.
Flesh: White, without scent, mild taste.
Habitat & distribution: From May to October, only on stumps of deciduous and coniferous trees; emerging either directly from wood or connected to it by thick, mycelial threads (rhizomorphs); frequent.

140 *Pluteus cervinus* ☺ Fawn Pluteus

Cap: Convex to flat; dark fawn; minutely scaly at centre when old; mostly 5-8 cm, rarely to 15 cm in diameter.
Gills: First white, later pale pink; crowded, free. *Spores:* Pink.
Stem: White; sometimes with brownish fibres or blotches.
Flesh: White; without scent, mild taste.
Habitat & distribution: On stumps of various deciduous and coniferous trees; mostly singly, occasionally on bark refuse, then in clusters and very numerous.
Similar species: *Pluteus atromarginatus* is darker with a black-brown edge to its gills.

left
136
right
137
138
left
139
right
140

141 *Collybia maculata* ☠ Spotted Tough-Shank

Cap: Convex when young, soon irregularly contorted; at first pure white, later developing rusty-red spots, can be evenly rusty-red when old; dry and smooth; up to over 10 cm in diameter.
Gills: White; very crowded, deeply sinuate; with strongly serrate edge.
Spores: White.
Stem: White, developing rusty-coloured spots; evenly thick, bare and occasionally twisted; distinctly striped; base often swollen obesely and rooting deeply in soil.
Flesh: White; very tough; bitter taste, without scent.
Habitat & distribution: Mostly around stumps in coniferous forests; in rows and often in clusters.
Similar species: The cap of *Collybia distorta* is red-brown from the start and irregularly contorted; its gills are very crowded, serrate and become spotted red-brown later; its stem is white, boldly longitudinally striped and twisted.

142 *Limacella glioderma* ☠ Slimy Veil Limacella

Cap: Convex when young, later flat; deep rustbrown at first, becoming pale later; very slimy; to 6 cm, rarely 12 cm in diameter.
Gills: Yellowish-white; thin, crowded and slightly adnate. *Spores:* White.
Stem: With woolly, patchy ring-like zone, encircled by reddish scales below; slender and evenly thick.
Flesh: White; mild taste, with strong, mealy smell.
Habitat & distribution: Singly or in groups, in deciduous and coniferous forests; fairly rare.
Similar species: Limacella guttata is larger and has a lighter, flesh-brown cap and a membranous ring which is covered in water droplets; when these dry up, they leave greyish-brown spots behind.

143 *Volvariella gloiocephala* ☠

Cap: Bell-shaped when young, later flatter; ivory-white with light grey centre; very slippery; to 12 cm in diameter.
Gills: White when young, later dirty pink; rather broad and moderately crowded, free. *Spores:* Pink.
Stem: White; rather long and slender, ring absent; somewhat bulbous at base, white volva reaching deep underground.
Flesh: White; mild taste.
Habitat & distribution: Mostly in fields, but also on meadows, parks and churchyards; fairly rare, but occasionally quite communal.
In some years the fungus grows in large enough quantities to be used as winter conserves. In older books on fungi it is occasionally recorded as poisonous.
Similar species: The volvariellas are closely related to the amanitas (152, 153, 154); they have free gills which are flushed pink with spores when old; like the bulbous agarics, their base covered by a membranous volva. However, most species of *Volvariella* are substantially smaller; the colour of their cap varies between white and dark grey.

141
142
143

144 *Amanita fulva* ☺ Tawny Grisette

Cap: Egg-shaped when young and entirely enveloped by the universal veil which is white on the inside and externally pale red-brown, later convex to flat, can be bowl-shaped when old; evenly orange-brown with a narrow, lighter striped margin; to 8 cm in diameter.
Gills: White; very crowded, free. *Spores:* White.
Stem: White; rather long and slender, gradually increasing in width from apex to base, ring absent, mostly covered in minute, concolorous tufts, base clothed in a brownish membranous volva; hollow.
Flesh: White; without scent, mild taste.
Habitat & distribution: Mostly in large numbers in deciduous and coniferous forests, in moist places, also on moors; frequent.
Similar species: Amanita fulva, A. battarrae (145) and *A. crocea* represent a section within the genus *Amanita* distinguished by the absence of a ring. All species of this group have a striped margin from immaturity. *A. crocea* is slightly larger and lighter orange-brown, with a snake-patterned stem. Distinguishing other, very closely related members of this group is difficult and they are sometimes looked upon only as varieties, not separate species. However, as all species are edible, their exact identification is only of scientific interest.
The edibility of *A. gemmata* is in dispute. It belongs to a different section within the genus *Amanita*, but loses its ring very early and then appears to be part of the above, ringless group. It has an orange-yellow cap, which is only occasionally indistinctly striped.

145 *Amanita battarrae*

Cap: Egg- to bell-shaped when young, later convex, can be flat when old; at first surrounded by a white, universal veil, later bare or with some larger shreds of veil remaining; at the apex dirty umber to olive-brown, towards the margin clearly striped from the start, much lighter and occasionally almost white; to 12 cm in diameter.
Gills: White; crowded, free. *Spores:* White.
Stem: Light greyish-brown or with yellowish snake pattern; strong, ring absent, gradually increasing in width towards base, volva deeply submerged in ground.
Flesh: White; mild taste, without scent.
Habitat & distribution: In coniferous forests, singly or in groups, mainly in mountain regions; rather frequent.
Similar species: The slightly larger *Amanita ceciliae* has similar colouration, but can be reddish- or yellowish-brown and frequently has the remains of a veil on the cap. It is not rare in deciduous and coniferous forests. There is a real danger of confusing these ringless fungi with the deadly poisonous bulbous agarics. Particularly when collecting young fruit bodies that are still surrounded by the universal veil and have a white margin, look out for the comb-like striped margin of the cap, to identify the ringless, edible group.

144

145

146 *Amanita phalloides* ☠ Death Cap

Cap: Acorn-shaped or hemispherical when young and surrounded by a white, egg shell-like universal veil, later convex and flat or somewhat bowl-shaped when old; mostly dark olive-green with a paler rim, but can also be lemon-yellow, yellow or pure white; slippery when young; up to 14 cm in diameter.
Gills: White, never changing to pink or grey; crowded, free. *Spores:* White.
Stem: Usually light olive green, with snake-like pattern; long, slender; ring is high, membranous, tearing easily and often attached to cap rim; base swollen, and enveloped by the remains of the volva.
Flesh: White; at first without scent, develops distinct sweet honey smell, when old has an unpleasant smell of ammonia.
Habitat & distribution: In deciduous woodland, mainly under oak and beech, not present at higher altitudes. The α-amanitin contained in the poisonous amanitas causes the destruction of the liver, and even small doses are fatal. The poison is active for years and cannot be destroyed by cooking – 50 g of fresh mushroom is fatal to a human being.
Similar species: White-capped *Agaricus campestris* (165), with which the fungus is confused frequently, have grey or pinkish-grey gills from the start and no volva. The margin of the cap in young specimens of *Amanita fulva* (144) and *A. battarrae* (145) is grooved.

147 *Amanita virosa* Destroying Angel

Cap: Young, egg-shaped and completely enclosed by the shell-like universal veil; later conical or convex, but never flat or funnel-shaped; pure white, somewhat brownish at apex when old; rather slippery when young; up to 10 cm in diameter.
Gills: White, never pink or grey; crowded, free. *Spores:* White.
Stem: White, rather long, with coarse white flocci; ring is near the top, membranous, tearing easily and often falling off or disappearing prematurely; base is swollen with a sack-like, white volva.
Flesh: White; with sweet, honey smell, as *Amanita phalloides*.
Habitat & distribution: Frequent, in groups in coniferous forests, particularly at higher altitudes; contains the same poisons as *A. phalloides*.
Similar species: There are no other gill fungi with a white cap, white gills, a ringed stem and a volva. However, this fungus is often mistaken for the similar species given under *A. phalloides*. We advise particular care when *Amanita fulva* (146) and *A. battarrae* (145) are collected. The caps of young forms of *A. battarrae* (145) often have a white margin and can only be distinguished by the grooves that become visible when the volva has been removed.

146

147

148 *Amanita citrina* ☠ False Death Cap

Cap: Hemispherical when young, soon convex or flat; light lemon-yellow, more rarely pure white; almost always with coarse, flaky remnants of the yellowish universal veil; to 8 cm in diameter.
Gills: White; crowded and free. *Spores:* White.
Stem: White; with persistent, hanging ring and a broad, pill box-like bulbous base without a volva.
Flesh: White; with smell of raw potatoes.
Habitat & distribution: Deciduous and coniferous forest; frequent.

149 *Amanita rubescens* ☺ The Blusher

Cap: Hemispherical when young, later evenly convex or flat; pale reddish-brown, more rarely off-white, yellowish-brown or reddish-grey; covered with dirty reddish-grey remains of universal veil, which can be wiped off; to 15 cm in diameter.
Gills: White, with reddish blotches when old; crowded, free. *Spores:* White.
Stem: White, clothed in minute flakes which redden later; widening gradually towards the base; with broad, hanging, white to yellowish, deeply grooved ring; bulbous base covered in warts.
Flesh: White, slowly reddening where damaged by grubs and when wounded.
Habitat & distribution: From June in deciduous and coniferous forests; frequent.
Use: One of the best culinary fungi; suitable for all methods of preparation; not for drying.
Similar species: There is a danger of confusing this fungus with the very poisonous *Amanita pantherina* (151). *A. rubescens* can vary enormously in appearance so can be hard to identify. Do not eat if you are in any doubt.

150 *Amanita muscaria* ☠ Fly Agaric

Cap: At first spherical and completely enveloped by a white, warty universal veil, later convex, flat or somewhat bowl-shaped with a grooved margin when old; bright orange-red to scarlet, lemon-yellow below the pellicle; up to 15 cm in diameter.
Gills: White, crowded, free. *Spores:* White.
Stem: White, evenly thick, with broad, hanging and comb-like grooved ring; bulbous base covered with the warty residues of veil.
Flesh: White; mild taste, no scent.
Habitat & distribution: In coniferous forests, mainly in pine plantations, often in groups; frequent.
Besides small amounts of muscarin, the fly agaric contains the agent muscimol which causes disturbances of consciousness and hallucinations. Do not try tasting this fungus. It contains further, not yet analysed poisons which are dangerous to health and can, in rare cases, prove fatal.
Similar species: The cap of *Amanita regalis* of highland forests is yellow- to dark-brown and yellow under the pellicle. Otherwise it is entirely similar to the fly agaric and is also poisonous.

148

149

150

151 *Amanita pantherina* ☠ The Panther

Cap: Hemispherical when young, later flat and frequently with comb-like grooves at margin; light buff to dark umber-brown; enveloped by a white universal veil when young; remnants of which remain as pure white, coarse warty tufts often arranged regularly around the margin.
Gills: White; crowded, free. *Spores:* White.
Stem: White; rather slender, with a narrow, smooth ring, which never has comb-like grooves; bulbous base bordered by warty remnants of veil.
Flesh: White, mild taste.
Habitat & distribution: In deciduous and coniferous woodlands; locally frequent; at higher altitudes forms lacking marginal grooves predominate. The poison acts like that of *A. phalloides*, but is stronger and can be fatal.

152 *Amanita porphyria* ☠

Cap: Almost spherical when young, later convex to flat; dark grey to brown; clothed in grey fibrous veil membrane remnants; to 8 cm in diameter.
Gills: White; crowded, free. *Spores:* White.
Stem: Whitish-grey; ring narrow, only indistinctly grooved and soon falling off; broad, bulbous base.
Flesh: White; smelling of radish.
Habitat & distribution: Mostly singly in coniferous forests; frequent.

153 *Amanita strobiliformis* ☺☒

Cap: Spherical when young, later convex; white pellicle covered with large, thick woolly shreds of universal veil; can grow to over 20 cm in diameter.
Gills: White; crowded. *Spores:* White.
Stem: White; thick; bulbous base deeply submerged in soil; ring soon splitting, coarsely floccose below the ring.
Flesh: White; weak smell of turnips.
Habitat & distribution: Mostly singly in deciduous forests and parks; fairly rare and should be protected.

154 *Amanita excelsa* ☺

Cap: Convex when young, later flat; whitish-grey or grey-brown to dark soot-grey; covered in pale grey, mostly connected veil remnants which can be wiped off; margin without grooves; to 12 cm in diameter.
Gills: White; crowded, free. *Spores:* White.
Stem: White; widening towards base; broad, hanging ring with comb-like grooves, with minutely grey, tufts below; indistinct bulbous base, with veil remnants towards the base.
Flesh: White; edible, mild but unpleasant taste; smell of turnip.
Habitat & distribution: From early summer in deciduous and coniferous forests; frequent.
Similar species: Danger of confusing *A. excelsa* with the very poisonous *A. pantherina* and the very rare and poisonous *A. regalis* which is distinguished from *A. excelsa* by its yellow pellicle.

151

left
152
right
153

154

155 *Macrolepiota procera* ☺ Parasol Mushroom

Cap: When very young, conical and uniformly dark red-brown; soon drumstick-shaped and splitting into coarse, woolly scales from the margin; smooth and later blunt umbonate at the centre; convex to flat when old; up to 30 cm in diameter.
Gills: White; broad and crowded, free; edge may turn brown with age.
Spores: White.
Stem: Splitting skin causes grey snake-pattern, very long, slender, bulbous base; broad, movable ring, white scales above, brown underneath, occasionally splitting prematurely; hollow.
Flesh: White; very tough and fibrous in the stem; mild taste, pleasant smell.
Habitat & distribution: Mostly in groups, in deciduous woodland, at waysides and in meadows; frequent.
Use: The caps can be fried like escalopes and are very tasty; can be poisonous if eaten raw.
Similar species: The giants of the genus *Macrolepiota* can be recognized by their movable ring. Some of the numerous, mostly much smaller parasol fungi of the genus *Lepiota* can attain the size of giant parasols, particularly *Lepiota acutesquamosa* (158), but they never have a ring that can be moved freely on the stem.

156 *Macrolepiota rhacodes* ☺ Shaggy Parasol

Cap: Spherical and light grey when young; soon splitting into flat, woolly, regularly arranged scales; apex dark brown and smooth; convex or flat when old, more rarely bowl-shaped or umbonate; up to 15 cm in diameter.
Gills: White, turning slightly brown when bruised; broad and rather crowded, free. *Spores:* White.
Stem: Evenly light greyish-brown, without snake pattern; long and slender, with a broad, bulbous base which compacts the needle litter it grows on; hollow; with broad, movable, fringed ring.
Flesh: White, turning slowly saffron-brown when damaged; mild taste, without scent.
Habitat & distribution: Mostly in groups in coniferous forests, among needle litter; frequent.
Use: As for parasol mushroom.
Similar species: The 'garden parasol' is a little darker brown and has a stronger, more funnel-shaped ring and an almost round bulbous base. It grows in gardens and is reportedly poisonous. Otherwise all giant parasols, recognisable by their freely movable ring, are edible. (See also the similar species for parasol mushroom.)

155

156

157 *Lepiota ignivolvata* ☠

Cap: Egg-shaped when young, soon convex to flat, often rather umbonate at apex; hazel-brown, lighter towards the rim and dissolving into ochre-brown small, flat scales; up to over 10 cm in diameter.
Gills: White; very crowded, free. *Spores:* White.
Stem: Fairly long; circled by an oblique, often incomplete zone, which has an orange-brown stripe.
Flesh: White; with a stinging, gassy smell.
Habitat & distribution: Mostly in groups in deciduous forests, predominantly in moist areas under beeches in deep leaf litter, rare.

158 *Lepiota acutesquamosa* ☠

Cap: Egg-shaped when young, later convex to flat; rust-brown at apex, covered mostly by dark, rust-brown warts towards the margin between which the white flesh of cap is visible; mostly 6-9 cm in diameter.
Gills: White; extremely crowded, frequently forked, free. *Spores:* White.
Stem: White apex, reddish-brown and scaly below the membranous, broad and hanging ring; evenly thick, slightly bulbous base.
Flesh: White; with unpleasant smell of gas.
Habitat & distribution: In deciduous and coniferous forests; frequent.
Similar species: The gills of *Lepiota perplexa* are not forked and it is far more rare.

159 *Macrolepiota mastoidea* ☺

Cap: First bell-shaped, soon convex or flat with small, nipple-like umbo; at the centre light fawn and minutely granular, there are flaky scales towards the margin which splits to show the white base below; mostly to 8 cm, seldom to 15 cm in diameter.
Gills: White; crowded, free. *Spores:* White.
Stem: Slender, bulbous, with slight snake-pattern and a broad, moveable ring.
Habitat & distribution: Mostly singly in deciduous woodland; fairly rare and should be protected.

160 *Lepiota cristata* ☠ Stinking Parasol

Cap: Bell-shaped when young, soon convex or flat; apex dark red to brownish-black, and with small, dark brown scales arranged in circles on a white background towards the margin; to 4 cm in diameter.
Gills: White; crowded. *Spores:* White.
Stem: White, reddening with age; the membranous ring soon falls off.
Flesh: White; with strong smell of coal gas.
Habitat & distribution: In large numbers in deciduous and coniferous forests, mainly along forest roads; very frequent.
Similar species: There are numerous small lepiotas with or without rings, some of which are very poisonous. None should be tasted. See p. 35 for pictures of similar lepiotas without rings.

157

left
158

right
159

160

161 *Cystoderma carcharias* ☠

Cap: First convex, can become flat, mostly broad and flat umbo; light flesh-brown and grainy with floccose margin; 3-5 cm in diameter.
Gills: White; crowded, deeply sinuate. *Spores:* White.
Stem: Evenly thick; apex bare; membranous and persistent ring which can be pulled off in downward movement; granular below ring.
Flesh: White; with unpleasant smell.
Habitat & distribution: Mostly late in the year and in large numbers; frequent.
Similar species: Cystoderma fallax is larger and more orange-brown; only in coniferous forests; fairly rare.

162 *Cystoderma terrei* ☠☒

Cap: Convex, can be flat when old; purple-red and evenly minutely granular; mostly 3-5 cm, rarely to 8 cm diameter.
Gills: White; very crowded, deeply sinuate. *Spores:* White.
Stem: Rust-red and floccose below the indistinct ring, which soon disappears; evenly thick or a little obese at the base.
Flesh: White; without scent or taste.
Habitat & distribution: In conifer forests, occasionally under deciduous trees or on rotten wood, mostly in groups; fairly rare and should not be picked.

163 *Cystoderma amianthinum* ☠ Saffron Parasol

Cap: Convex and often with a small, indistinct umbo, can be flat when old, sometimes a little wrinkly; light yellowish-brown, occasionally ochreous; finely granular; mostly 2-3 cm, rarely to 6 cm in diameter.
Gills: White, pale straw-coloured when old, crowded, sinuate.
Spores: White.
Stem: Evenly thick, with weakly bulbous base; usually rather long and often a little bent; apex bare, with indistinct ring, yellowish-brown with grainy scales below.
Flesh: Yellowish; with mouldy, unpleasant smell.
Habitat & distribution: Almost throughout the year in conifer forests; frequent.

164 *Cystoderma granulosum* ☠☒

Cap: First convex, later flat; bright orange to rust-red; finely granular, occasionally wrinkly and striped; to 4 cm diameter.
Gills: White; crowded, sinuate. *Spores:* White.
Stem: Long and slender, white, floccose ring soon disappearing; lovely rust-red and granular below.
Flesh: White or reddish; without scent.
Habitat & distribution: In small groups in coniferous forests; rare and should be protected.
Similar species: The genus *Cystoderma* is distinguished from that of *Lepiota* and *Macrolepiota* by an evenly fine grainy cover on the cap, which continues below the ring down to the base of the stem.

161

left
162
right
163

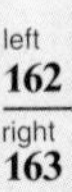

164

165 *Agaricus campestris* ☺ Field Mushroom

Cap: Hemispherical when young, later flat; white, when old occasionally becoming slightly greyish-brown and scaly, no discolouration when bruised; to 10 cm in diameter.
Gills: Never pure white; light greyish-pink at first, later purplish-brown to almost black; crowded, free. *Spores:* Dark red-brown.
Stem: Evenly thick, no bulbous base, rather short; with broad, hanging ring which soon disappears.
Flesh: White, weakly reddish discolouration where cut; scent pleasant, not of aniseed.
Habitat & distribution: Mostly in large numbers on meadows and pastures; locally frequent.
Use: Suitable for all recipes and can be prepared in any way, but has no characteristic flavour.
Similar species: There is anger of confusing A. *campestris* with the two deadly poisonous bulbous agarics A. *muscaria* and A. *pantherina*. Inexperienced collectors can confuse other white-capped fungi that grow in meadows, but sometimes look entirely different; *Volvariella gloiocephala* (143) for instance, with A. *campestris*. In similar habitats and often in domestic gardens grows the edible *Leucoagaricus pudicus* which looks deceptively similar to A. *campestris*, but has white gills which later become pale pink.

166 *Agaricus bitorquis* ☺ Pavement Mushroom

Cap: Hemispherical when young, with inrolled margin, later flat at the centre; first white, later slightly grey or ochreous; with firm flesh; to 10 cm in diameter.
Gills: Greyish-pink when young, later dark purple-brown; crowded, free. *Spores:* Purplish-brown.
Stem: White; short, with acute base and two separate rings.
Flesh: White, slightly reddening; with pleasant smell and mild taste.
Habitat & distribution: Mostly in groups, at roadsides among stone debris; can even lift tarmac; always outside forests.
Use: Just as A. *campestris*, but the flesh of this fungus is more firm and has a stronger taste.

167 *Agaricus sylvaticus* ☺ Scaly Wood Mushroom

Cap: Hemispherical when young, later flat; deep red to greyish-brown; covered with broad scales; to 10 cm in diameter.
Gills: Purple-grey when young, very dark when old; crowded, free. *Spores:* Purplish-brown
Stem: Brownish; often with a hanging ring and a small bulb at the base.
Flesh: White, turning red when cut; mild taste.
Habitat & distribution: From early summer, in groups in coniferous forests; frequent.
Use: Young fruit bodies are suitable for all recipes.
Similar species: Tricholoma vaccinum (127) looks similar from above but has no ring and has white, later reddish-brown, gills. A. *haemorrhoidarius* is distinguished by its flesh which turns immediately red when cut.

165

166

167

168 *Agaricus macrosporus* ☺

Cap: First hemispherical, later convex to flat; white, slowly becoming yellow when bruised; with fine silky scales; 25-50 cm in diameter.
Gills: Grey when young, later purplish-brown, crowded, free.
Spores: Purplish-brown.
Stem: Strong and very thick, rather short; with very broad and thick ring; initially this juts out horizontally, its dentate rim resembling a cog; yellowish and floccose below.
Flesh: White, turning slowly orange or red in the cut stem; mild taste, smell of aniseed.
Habitat & distribution: From June at wood fringes and in meadows; rare.
Similar species: There is danger of confusing A. *macrosporus* with the deadly poisonous bulbous agarics A. *phalloides* (146), A. *muscaria* (150) and A. *pantherina* (151).

169 *Agaricus abruptibulbus* ☺

Cap: At first hemispherical, later broadly convex or flat; first pure white, finely silky, occasionally also floccose; thin flesh, which discolours yellow immediately when touched; when old, often watery purple, sometimes yellow; to 12 cm in diameter.
Gills: Initially purplish-grey, almost black when old, crowded, free.
Spores: Purplish-grey.
Stem: White; rather long, strong, with broad, membranous, hanging ring, with a small bulb at base.
Flesh: White, not discolouring when cut; smelling of aniseed.
Habitat & distribution: In groups in conifer forests; frequent.
Use: Suitable, in spite of the strong aniseed smell, as a mushroom vegetable and for salads; contains high concentration of heavy metals (cadmium). Beware confusion with the deadly poisonous bulbous agarics.
Similar species: Agaricus silvicola which grows in deciduous and coniferous forests is very similar, but the flesh of its cap is even thinner. *Agaricus arvensis* (horse mushroom) grows in meadows has no bulb.

170 *Agaricus xanthoderma* ☠

Cap: Hemispherical when young, later convex; at first pure white, later discolouring pale greyish-brown and sometimes breaking up into coarse, thick scales, but usually staying smooth, yellowing when bruised; to 10 cm in diameter.
Gills: Pink when young, later increasingly dark chocolate-brown; crowded, free. *Spores:* Purplish-brown.
Stem: Rather long and slender, smooth; with membranous ring, floccose below; distinctly bulbous base.
Flesh: White, discolouring vividly chrome-yellow in base if bruised; mostly without scent when fresh; smelling unpleasantly of carbolic or ink when old and particularly on boiling.
Habitat & distribution: Mostly in larger groups on forest fringes, in parks and meadows; rather frequent.
Agaricus xanthoderma should not be eaten as it causes violent vomiting immediately, though does not damage health permanently.

168

169

170

171 *Oudemansiella mucida* ☠ Slimy Beech Caps

Cap: Hemispherical when young, later evenly convex; white to light grey; slightly striped, thickly covered with translucent slime, thin-skinned; with striped margin when old; to 6 cm in diameter, rarely larger.
Gills: White; thick, distant, with a waxy appearance. *Spores:* White.
Stem: White or light grey; rather stiff, with broad ring grooved on top.
Flesh: White; without scent.
Habitat & distribution: On the wood of beech or oak, on moist branches or trunks on the ground; locally frequent.

172 *Panaeolus fimiputris* ☠

Cap: Egg- or bell-shaped, light clay-coloured, slippery and glossy; to 4 cm in diameter.
Gills: Greyish-black, blotchy; black with white edge when old; crowded.
Spores: Black.
Stem: Whitish-grey; with small bulbous base; ringed below centre, hollow.
Habitat & distribution: Exclusively on cow-pats; frequent on highland pastures.

173 *Stropharia aeruginosa* ☠ Verdigris Toadstool

Cap: Bell-shaped when young, later convex to flat; at first dark bluish-green and with white tufts that swim on the detachable slimy cover, later growing pale to a light ochre-yellow when old; to 6 cm in diameter.
Gills: Whitish-grey, later purplish-grey; fairly crowded; with white, floccose edge. *Spores:* Purplish-black.
Stem: Light, blue-green skin with a grooved ring, the top side of which is dusted purplish-black by spores; with white flocci below the ring-zone, becoming bare later.
Flesh: White, greenish in the stem; without scent; slightly bitter taste when old.
Habitat & distribution: In deciduous and coniferous forests; predominantly in moist places; frequent.
Similar species: Stropharia caerulea, a common species which is usually overlooked; it has the same cap colour, but with brownish gills with a less strongly floccose edge; the stem is hardly floccose and has a ring only briefly.

174 *Stropharia hornemannii* ☠☒

Cap: First convex, then flat; violet-grey to light chestnut-brown and very slimy; margin has white tufts at first; to 15 cm in diameter.
Gills: White-grey, later violet-grey; crowded. *Spores:* Grey-black.
Stem: Rather long, evenly thick; ring membranous, often falls off when old; with white flocci below ring.
Flesh: White; with unpleasant smell and taste.
Habitat & distribution: On and around highly decayed conifer stumps, rare at lower altitudes; may be poisonous, so should not be eaten.
Similar species: Stropharia rugosa-annulata, which grows in ploughed fields, is larger and has yellow- to red-brown caps. Very rare in the wild, it can easily be grown and is offered as 'brown-cap' for home cultivation.

171

left
172
right
173

174

175 *Catathelasma imperiale* ☺☒ Imperial Cap

Cap: Hemispherical when young, later convex, more rarely flat at centre with long inrolled margin; light chestnut-brown to fawn, with bold marbled stripes; may be covered in white remnants of veil when young; thick flesh; to 20 cm in diameter.
Gills: White; very narrow, rather crowded, slightly decurrent when old.
Spores: White.
Stem: Very thick and strong, hard flesh; with white apex and two separate, narrow rings which come off when pulled; slightly brown towards base and narrowing like a turnip.
Flesh: White, noticeably heavy, very mealy smell, mild taste.
Habitat & distribution: Growing singly in conifer forests on chalk, fairly rare, more frequent in mountains; should be protected.

176 *Phaeolepiota aurea* ☺

Cap: At first hemispherical, later convex or flat, usually with blunt umbo; lovely yellow- to orange-brown; finely grained or velvety, occasionally striped, thick flesh; to 20 cm in diameter.
Gills: Light rust-brown; crowded, free. *Spores:* Rust-brown.
Stem: Thick, swollen somewhat club-like at base; with light yellow apex; ring very broad and membranous, yellowish-brown and granular below, can be removed if pulled downwards; below ring yellowish-brown, with flaky grains.
Flesh: White or yellowish; mild taste.
Habitat & distribution: At waysides, in parks; fairly rare.
Paeolepiota aurea is among the most beautiful European fungi. In spite of its rust-brown spores it is put into the lepiota group.

177 *Rozites caperatus* ☺ Gypsy Mushroom

Cap: Hemispherical when young, later convex, flat or somewhat bowl-shaped when old; at first with glossy, pale violet pruinose cover, which is soon lost in moist weather, light honey-brown below that, wrinkly when old; to 10 cm in diameter.
Gills: Light milk-coffee-brown, crowded, slightly wrinkly and bent, with edge finely serrated, sinuate. *Spores:* Rust-brown.
Stem: Evenly thick with abrupt base and white floccose apex; with a narrow, membranous ring in the middle, which is visible below the cap of the young fungus.
Flesh: Pale brownish and marbled; without scent, mild taste.
Habitat & distribution: Often communally in acid conifer forests, mainly with bilberries; rather frequent.
Use: One of the tastiest edible mushrooms; particularly suitable for use as a vegetable and with meat.
Similar species: Numerous cortinarias resemble *R. caperatus* in their shape and cap colour, but their stem has no ring. When very young, pruinose *R. caperatus* fungi are collected, they can be confused with young *Cortinarius traganus* (223). These often grow in similar places but are inedible.

175

176

177

178 *Armillaria mellea* ☺ Honey Fungus

Cap: Convex when young, later flat; dark scales over a honey-coloured, rarely olive-brown skin, later with striped margin; mostly 5-10 cm in diameter.
Gills: At first cream, soon light brown and blotchy; crowded, decurrent.
Spores: White.
Stem: With narrow ring which is yellowish or red-brown and scaly below; the base is usually obese.
Flesh: Brownish; without scent, mild taste.
Habitat & distribution: In clusters on the dead wood of deciduous and coniferous trees; frequent; can also attack living trees.
If the fungus is not cooked thoroughly, it can cause gastric complaints for delicate stomachs.

179 *Kuehneromyces mutabilis* ☺

Two-toned wood-tuft or Two-toned Pholiota

Cap: At first convex with inrolled margin, soon flat and usually with blunt umbo; honey-brown when moist and slightly slippery with striped margin, becoming paler when dry and discolouring to light yellow-brown from the centre; to 5 cm in diameter.
Gills: Whitish when young, soon pale cinnamon-brown; crowded.
Spores: Rust-brown.
Stem: Long and bent, hollow, often grooved at apex; the ring is usually rolled up and coloured rust-brown by spores; below the ring there are numerous small lighter scales on a brown back ground; bare when old.
Flesh: Brownish; without mealy smell, mild taste.
Habitat & distribution: From May to October always in clusters on deciduous tree stumps, also on conifers in mountainous areas; frequent everywhere.
Use: The caps are suitable for flavouring soups and sauces.
Similar species: There is a danger of confusing *K. mutabilis* with the very poisonous *Galerina marginata* (180).

180 *Galerina marginata* ☠

Cap: Bell-shaped when young, later almost flat; when moist honey-brown with translucent margin striped by gills, wit greasy gloss, when dry yellowish-brown; mostly 2-4 cm in diameter.
Gills: Pale rust-brown; thin and crowded. *Spores:* Rust-brown.
Stem: Long and slender; pruinose at apex, with membranous ring which is not rolled in, but often falls off; floccose or fibrous below ring; black-brown discolouration starts at the base; hollow.
Flesh: Brownish, mild taste, with mealy smell.
Habitat & distribution: Mostly on lawns, but also in clusters on remnants of coniferous wood, on fallen trunks and stumps, occasionally on beech wood; frequent.
The fungus contains a dangerous amount of α-amanitin, the poison of the bulbous agarics, and consumption can be fatal.
Similar species: The edible *Kuehneromyces mutabilis* (179) resembles *Galerina marginata* so closely, that the species can often be distinguished only by their smell. Confusion is also possible with *Flammulina velutipes*, which is distinguished by no having a ring, and by growing in winter.

178

179

180

181 *Hypholoma fsciculare* ☠ Sulphur Tuft

Cap: First convex, later expanded; orange-brown with sulphur-yellow, occasionally greenish-yellow, margin; to 5 cm in diameter.
Gills: First sulphur-yellow, soon greenish, grey-green when old; rather narrow, sinuate, dense. *Spores:* Dark brown.
Stem: Sulphur-yellow, with fibrous ring zone, somewhat scaly below when young, later turning brownish.
Flesh: Light sulphur-yellow; very bitter; consumption causes gastric complaints.
Habitat & distribution: From May on stumps of deciduous trees, occasionally on conifer wood; frequent.

182 *Hypoloma capnoides* ☺

Cap: Hemispherical, later convex, often uneven; at first yellow, later with orange-brown hues at the apex; 3-6 cm in diameter.
Gills: White at first, soon purple-grey, never yellow or green; crowded, sinuate. *Spores:* dark brown.
Stem: Yellow, turning rusty-brown from base upward; occasionally has fibrous ring zone when young, with silky fibres below, bare when old.
Flesh: Yellowish-white; with pleasant smell, mild taste.
Habitat: Throughout year, in dense clusters on conifer stumps; frequent.
Use: As *Kuehneromyces mutabilis*, two-toned Pholiota (100).
Similar species: Can be confused with *Hypholoma fasciculare* (181).

183 *Gymnopilus penetrans* ☠

Cap: Convex; pale yellow, can be golden yellow at the apex; bare and smooth; up to 5 cm in diameter.
Gills: Light yellow when young, later rust-brown, blotchy; narrow, crowded, sinuate. *Spores:* Rust-brown.
Stem: Yellow; slightly fibrous; evenly thick, without ring, often with white mesh of fungal threads at the base.
Flesh: Off white, ochre-yellow in the stem; no scent, bitter.
Habitat & distribution: Clusters rare, but often numerous on stumps and branches of various conifers; frequent.

184 *Hypholoma sublateritium*

Brick-red Hypholoma

Cap: Convex when young, later flat; bright brick-red to orange, towards the margin paler redish-yellow and often with small, white, fibrous scales; up to 8 cm in diameter.
Gills: Yellowish-white when young, later dark olive-grey to brown; crowded and sinuate. *Spores:* Olive purple-brown.
Stem: Orange to rust-brown, first with fibrous ring zone, scaly below.
Flesh: White, yellowish in the stem; bitter taste.
Habitat & distribution: In clusters on stumps of various deciduous and coniferous trees; frequent.
Similar species: The cap of *Pholiota astragalina* has a similar colour, but its gills are first yellow and later olive-yellow. It is found only on conifer stumps in mountain regions.

181

left
182
right
183

184

185 *Inocybe rimosa* ☠

Cap: A pointed cone when young, later expanded, but always pointed umbonate, strongly fibrous, tearing from the rim; pale straw-coloured, more rarely grey-brown or lemon-yellow; to 5 cm in diameter.
Gills: First whitish-grey, later dirty grey-olive; edge with white flocci.
Spores: Tobacco-brown.
Stem: White; slightly pruinose. *Flesh:* Mealy.
Habitat & distribution: In deciduous and coniferous forests, along waysides; frequent.
This fungus contains muscarin and consumption can be fatal.

186 *Inocybe geophylla* Common White Inocybe

Cap: Egg-shaped when young, later broadly bell-shaped with small umbo; white, rarely brownish or a lovely violet; up to 3 cm in diameter.
Gills: First white, soon clay-coloured; edge a little floccose.
Spores: Tobacco-brown.
Stem: White; without bulbous base. *Flesh:* Mealy.
Habitat & distribution: In deciduous and coniferous forests, mainly along waysides; very frequent.
This fungus has a high content of muscarin and is very poisonous; consumption can be fatal.

187 *Inocybe asterospora* ☠

Cap: First conical, later convex, broadly umbonate, with even, radial splits, margin tears when old; dark chestnut-brown, 3 to 6 cm in diameter.
Gills: Young whitish-grey, cinnamon-brown when old.
Spores: Tobacco-brown; seen under a microscope spores are star-shaped.
Stem: Light red-brown, apex white, pruinose; bulbous base. *Flesh:* Mealy.
Habitat & distribution: In deciduous and coniferous forests; infrequent.

188 *Inocybe maculata* ☠

Cap: Pointed umbonate when young, later broadly bell-shaped or flat with strong umbo; splitting from the margin; deep umber with whitish-grey spots at centre; up to 4 cm in diameter.
Gills: First white-grey then olive-brown; usually crowded, deeply sinuate.
Spores: dark brown.
Stem: Rather light at first, slightly pruinose at apex; turning brown when old; long and slender. *Flesh:* White; mealy.
Habitat & distribution: Among grass and in forests; frequent.

189 *Inocybe phaeodisca* ☠☒

Cap: First bell-shaped, often with umbo, then expanded, light red-brown at centre; with fibrous scales near the white rim; to 2 cm in diameter.
Gills: First pale ochre, then cinnamon; crowded, light, with minutely floccose edge. *Spores:* dark brown.
Stem: Pink-brown, slender, often bent. *Flesh:* White; mild, no scent.
Habitat & distribution: Moist, deciduous woods, locally frequent, otherwise rare.

left
185

right
186

187

left
188

right
189

190 *Cortinarius bicolor* ☠ ☒

Cap: Bell-shaped when young, expanding later, with indistinct blunt umbo; violet-brown and moist when young, later dark chestnut brown, fawn when dry; to 5 cm in diameter.
Gills: Lilac when young, soon dark rust-brown, thick, very distant and broad, sinuate. *Spores:* Rust-brown.
Stem: Evenly blue-lilac; longitudinally fibrous; can have white, ring-like zones towards base; rather long, cylindrical or attenuate.
Flesh: Watery lilac-brown, distinct smell of radish.
Habitat & distribution: Groups, mostly in moist coniferous forests. occasionally in deciduous woodland; fairly rare, should be protected.

191 *Cortinarius strobilaceus* ☠

Cap: At first bell-shaped, later flat, rather pointed umbo; dark hazel-brown when moist, dirty yellowish-brown when dry, densely covered in small, yellowish scales; to 4 cm in diameter.
Gills: Dark yellow-brown, rather thick, a little distant.
Spores: Rust-brown.
Stem: Concolorous with cap; with woolly, floccose belts; very long, slender.
Habitat & distribution: In groups in coniferous, rarely deciduous, forests, mainly at higher altitudes, rather frequent.

192 *Cortinarius paleaceus* ☠

Cap: Bell-shaped when young, later flat, usually with strong, pointed umbo; dark grey-brown to umber when moist, sometimes with lilac tints; mostly light yellowish-brown when dry, densely covered in small pointed white or brown scales, rarely bare; up to 3 cm in diameter.
Gills: Yellowish-brown, rather crowded. *Spores:* Rusty-brown.
Stem: Grey-brown, with a white ring-zone, below this it has white flocci; long, slender.
Flesh: Dark grey-brown; when squashed distinct smell of geranium.
Habitat & distribution: In groups in deciduous and coniferous woods, very frequent in moist pine woods.

193 *Cortinarius renidens* ☠

Cap: Convex when young, later flat; bright orange when moist, turning pale apricot-yellow, beginning at apex; to 5 cm in diameter.
Gills: Vivid rust-orange, broad and thick, moderately crowded.
Spores: Rusty-brown.
Stem: Light orange-brown, longitudinally fibrous; evenly thick or attenuated; ring-zone indistinct or absent.
Flesh: Watery orange-brown; mild taste.
Habitat & distribution: In groups, sometimes clustering, in coniferous forests, mainly in clearings and among grass; rather rare.
Similar species: In *Cortinarius armeniacus* the cap looks just as vivid, but the stem is white. It is somewhat larger and also grows in conifer forests.

190

left **191**

right **192**

193

194 *Cortinarius cinnabarinus* ☠

Cap: Broadly bell-shaped; bright cinnabar-red, when old and moist also darker blood- or brown-red; up to 5 cm in diameter.
Gills: Cinnabar-red when young, later with rusty-brown sheen, rather crowded. *Spores:* Rusty-brown.
Stem: Cinnabar-red; long and slender, somewhat fibrous.
Flesh: Vivid cinnabar-red throughout; with earthy smell.
Habitat & distribution: Mostly in small groups in deciduous woodland mainly below beeches; rare.
Similar species: Cortinarius anthracinus grows in fenland forests. Cap is darker blackish-red, almost black when moist, carmine at margin.

195 *Cortinarius semisanguineus* ☠

Cap: Bell-shaped when young, soon flat and usually with a small, broad umbo; light hazel-brown, with minute olive-brown scales; to 5 cm in diameter.
Gills: At first blood-red, then rusty-red and pruinose, rather crowded
Spores: Rust-brown
Stem: Vivid brass-coloured to yellow, longitudinally fibrous, often rather bent
Flesh: Yellowish-brown, yellow in stem; with earthy smell.
Habitat & distribution: In groups in coniferous forests, mostly among moss with bilberries; also in bogs; rather frequent.
Similar species: Cortinarius croceus has similar cap shape and colour, but lemon-yellow gills; it grows in deciduous and coniferous woods; frequent.

196 *Cortinarius sanguineus* ☠

Cap: Hemispherical when young, later flat or contorted; first dark blood-red, blackish-red when old; minutely scaly; 2-4 cm in diameter.
Gills: Dark blood-red with a rust-brown dust of spores.
Stem: Blood-red with lighter red fibres, background sometimes orange-red ; evenly thick, mostly long and slender.
Flesh: Blood-red throughout; usually with weak, earthy smell.
Habitat & distribution: Singly or in small groups in moist conifer forests and bogs; quite frequent.

197 *Cortinaria cinnamomeus* ☠

Cap: Hemispherical when young, later flat, broad, very blunt umbonate; at first hazel-brown, later dark umber, often with an olive hue; somewhat felty; 3-5 cm in diameter.
Gills: When young bright cinnamon-orange to saffron-yellow, tending to rust-brown when old; moderately crowded. *Spores:* rust-brown.
Stem: Yellowish-green, often with brown fibres at the base; evenly thick and rather long.
Flesh: Light greenish-yellow; with weakly earthy smell.
Habitat & distribution: Mostly in groups in coniferous forests; more rarely under deciduous trees; not rare.
Similar species: The fairly rare *Cortinarius malicorius* has a more cinnamon-brown cap with an orange to saffron-coloured margin and more vividly fire-coloured gills.

194

left
195
right
196

197

198 *Panaeolus papilionaceus* ☠

Cap: Bell-shaped, margin floccose, later bare, somewhat wrinkly and dark brown-grey to clay-coloured; to 3 cm wide and equally high.
Gills: First grey, soon black with light, floccose edge. *Spores:* black.
Stem: Initially white, later black and pruinose; often contorted.
Habitat & distribution: Only on cowpats, on pasture land; frequent.

199 *Panaeolus foenisecii* ☠

Cap: Hemispherical to bell-shaped; dark purplish-brown when moist, clay-coloured when dry; to 3 cm in diameter.
Gills: Light rust-coloured with floccose edge, later dark rust-brown and blotchy. *Spores:* Purplish-brown.
Stem: Pale flesh-brown, with silky gloss; long and very thin.
Habitat & distribution: On freshly mown meadows and lawns; frequent after rain.

200 *Melanophyllum haematospermum* ☠

Cap: Convex; dark brown-grey and floccose, fringed margin; 2-3 cm diam.
Gills: Dark blood-red; crowded; greenish when fresh, rust-brown when old.
Habitat & distribution: Along waysides among grass and nettles; rare.

201 *Stropharia semiglobata* Dung Roundhead

Cap: Hemispherical; light yellow, slippery; to 3 cm in diameter.
Gills: Whitish-grey when young, dark olive-grey when old with light, floccose edge. *Spores:* Purplish-brown.
Stem: Ochre-yellow; rather long, evenly thick; ring disappears fast, but often entirely absent; sticky below.
Habitat & distribution: On manured spots; on old cowpats; frequent.

202 *Coprinus disseminatus* ☠ Trooping Crumble Cap

Cap: Bell-shaped, very dainty and striped; whitish-grey, not dissolving; to 1 cm in diameter.
Gills: Grey, almost black when old, thin and rather distant. *Spores:* Black.
Stem: White; somewhat translucent, very thin, frail, weakly mealy.
Habitat & distribution: From May, forms dense lawns, on stumps and at the base of living trees; frequent.

203 *Coprinus xanthotrix* ☠

Cap: First egg-shaped, later expanded; ochre-yellow at the centre, near margin whitish-grey and furrowed; white and shaggy when young, thin-skinned and very short-lived; to 4 cm in diameter.
Gills: Soon turning grey-black, crowded. *Spores:* Black.
Stem: White; rather long, with white tufts when young.
Habitat & distribution: On moist soil in deciduous woodland, rarely on wood; not rare.

left
198
right
199

left
200
right
201

left
202
right
203

204 *Coprinus micaceus* ☠ Glistening Ink Cap

Cap: Egg-shaped when young, later bell-shaped; yellow- to foxy-brown; grooved, small glistening grains cover apex of young cap and soon disappear; up to 3 cm wide and equally high.
Gills: Greyish-white, later black with lighter, floccose edge. *Spores:* Black.
Stem: White; ring absent.
Habitat & distribution: From May in groups on moist soil or stumps; frequent.

205 *Coprinus atramentarius* ☠

Cap: At first egg-shaped, then broadly bell-shaped; light grey-brown, grooved, floccose and pruinose at apex when young; to 7 cm high and wide.
Gills: First whitish-grey, later black. *Spores:* black.
Stem: Evenly thick, with ring-like remains of the veil at the base.
Flesh: White; without scent, mild taste.
Habitat & distribution: Gardens, waysides, in forests only at roads; frequent.
Coprinus atramentarius contains coprin which is poisonous only in connection with alcohol. Under no circumstances must any alcohol, in whatever form, be taken for 1-2 days before or after consumption.

206 *Coprinus comatus* ☺ Shaggy Ink Cap

Cap: Acorn-shaped when young, white with light brown, smooth apex with recurved floccose scales, later turning up from the rim, pink, then black, deliquescent from the margin; to 5 cm wide, 8 cm high.
Gills: White when young, at first purplish-red from the margin, then later black and slowly dissolving. *Spores:* Black.
Stem: White; rather strong, ring positioned low, soon falling off.
Flesh: White; mild taste, pleasant smell.
Habitat & distribution: On manured meadows, rubble, lawns and gardens; frequent.
Use: Its very mild aroma is unique. Young mushrooms are particularly suited to use as a vegetable. Use straight after collection. Discolouring or deliquescent fungi should not be eaten.

207 *Coprinus picaceus* ☠ Magpie Ink Cap

Cap: In shape as *C. comatus* (206), but dark date-brown with whitish-grey (non-scaly) patches; deliquescent when old.
Gills: First whitish-grey then black and deliquescent. *Spores:* Black.
Stem: As in shaggy ink cap (206), but without ring.
Habitat & distribution: Singly in deciduous woods, under beech; uncommon.

208 *Psathyrella piluliformis* ☠

Cap: Convex; red-brown when moist, turning very pale and clay-coloured when dry; sometimes a little striped; to 4 cm in diameter.
Gills: Pale brown, later chocolate-brown; crowded. *Spores:* Colour as gills.
Stem: First white, turning brown later, white and felty at base.
Flesh: White; very brittle, without scent, mild taste.
Habitat & distribution: Communally in moist places or at burnt sites, less on stumps; frequent.

left
204

right
205

206

left
207

right
208

209 *Pholiota squarrosa* ☠ Shaggy Pholiota

Cap: First convex, later expanded, occasionally flat; dense, rough, brown scales on a light straw-coloured to orange-brown base, recurved at tip; up to 6 cm, rarely to 12 cm in diameter.
Gills: When young waxy-yellow, later increasingly rust-brown; narrow and crowded; sinuate when young, later somewhat decurrent.
Spores: Dark brown.
Stem: At the apex yellow and bare, with a fibrous veil connected to the margin of cap when young; covered in rough, rust-brown scales on lower stem; evenly thick.
Flesh: Dirty yellow with radish-like smell and somewhat bitter taste.
Habitat & distribution: On stumps and at the base of living trees, mostly on coniferous, rarely on deciduous trees; frequent.
Similar species: The fungus is often confused with *Armillaria mellea* (178), the honey fungus which is of similar size and appears in the same season. However, the stem of *A. mellea* is ringed, and it never has such rough scales on the stem or cap.

210 *Pholiota flammans* ☠ Kummer Cap

Cap: Convex with small umbo when young, later flat; bright lemon-yellow to orange, densely covered in concolorous, pointed, upright scales; 3-6 cm, rarely to 10 cm in diameter.
Gills: A vivid yellow when young, later light rust-brown; crowded, sinuate. *Spores:* Ochre-brown.
Stem: Sulphur-yellow, with fibrous, almost ring-like zone, and densely covered below with concolorous, rough scales.
Flesh: Lemon-yellow, later brownish; weak radish-like smell, bitter.
Habitat & distribution: In tufts on conifer stumps, in moist and shady areas; rather frequent.
Similar species: Among the pholiotas there are species with a dry, rough-scaled cap and some with a slimy cap. In the slimy species; white or dark flocci tend to swim near the margin and then either disappear or stick to the cap. Almost all pholiotas grow on wood. The red pholiota *P. astragalina* also grows in clusters on conifer wood and has similar, deeper, fire-orange colours, no scales, but rather a smooth, dry cap which is paler towards the margin; its gills are more ochre-yellow and decurrent over a short span.

209

210

211 *Pholiota aurivella (P. cerifera)* ☠

Golden Pholiota

Cap: Convex when young, later flat; bright orange-yellow with a foxy-brown apex; at first very slimy and covered with small, darker scales, later drying up; to 12 cm in diameter.
Gills: Light yellow when young, later brown and frequently with olive hues; crowded, sinuate. *Spores:* Brown.
Stem: Light yellow-brown; with floccose fibres, not slimy; ring absent, rarely with indistinct ring-zone.
Habitat & distribution: Mostly in clusters on stumps and wounds of living trees, predominantly on deciduous wood, also in mountainous areas on coniferous wood; often appearing only late in the year; not rare.
Similar species: Pholiota adiposa which also grows in clusters on deciduous wood. Its cap, when young, is more sulphur-yellow and its stem is slimy. *P. lucifera* is smaller, light lemon-yellow with fading scales; it grows in dense clusters in woodlands and meadows, always on pieces of wood covered in soil.

212 *Pholiota lenta* ☠

Cap: Hemispherical when young, with inrolled margin, later broadly convex; pale clay-coloured; very slimy, when young white flocci swim in slime at margin; to 6 cm in diameter.
Gills: Whitish straw-coloured when young, later pale clay-coloured; crowded, somewhat sinuate, decurrent when old. *Spores:* Brown.
Stem: White; floccose and scaly, turning brown; evenly thick.
Flesh: Pale, brownish; with weak smell of radish.
Habitat & distribution: In groups, not clusters; on leaf litter from deciduous and coniferous trees; also frequent on pieces of wood.
Similar species: The larger *Pholiota lubrica* is more of a foxy-brown, its cap is very slimy, white flocci swim in the slime at its margin; it grows mostly in groups on moist spots on wood of deciduous trees; its flesh smells weakly of radish; the gills are whitish-grey when young, later greenish-yellow.

213 *Pholiota populnea* ☠

Cap: Hemispherical when young and erupting from wood as a round, tuberous shape, with inrolled, fibrous margin, later convex, more rarely umbonate; has a dense and even cover of whitish-grey, woolly scales on pale clay-brown background which is rust-brown at the centre; to 20 cm in diameter.
Gills: Almost white when young, later dark cinnamon-brown; broad, crowded; sinuate when young, a little decurrent when old. *Spores:* Ochre.
Stem: Pale brownish with some white scales; short and thick with a tuberous, rooting base.
Flesh: White, cinnamon-brown at base of stem; with aromatic scent.
Habitat & distribution: On stumps and felled trunks of poplars; rather rare.

211

212

213

214 *Hebeloma crustuliniforme* ☠

Fairy Cake Hebeloma

Cap: First convex, later flat and often irregularly contorted; light clay-coloured to grey-ochre when young, paler when old; slippery when moist, glossy when dry; up to 8 cm in diameter.
Gills: Whitish-grey when young, later darker cinnamon brown; crowded, floccose at the edge with water droplets which are only visible under a microscope. *Spores:* Grey-brown.
Stem: Yellowish-white and covered with white flocci when young, later bare; evenly thick or somewhat bulbous at the base.
Flesh: White; with strong radish smell; causes gastric problems when consumed.
Habitat & distribution: From September usually very numerous; in clusters and fairy rings in deciduous and coniferous forests, by woodland fringes and in undergrowth; frequent.
Similar species: There are a number of other Hebeloma species that are difficult to distinguish. *Pholiota lenta* (212) is also similar; it is distinguished by having white flocci that swim in its cap-slime.

215 *Hebeloma sinapizans* ☠

Cap: First convex, later flat; light reddish-brown, margin paler; very slippery when moist, pruinose when dry; up to 15 cm in diameter.
Gills: Light grey when young, later coffee-brown; rather crowded and deeply sinuate near stem. *Spores:* Greyish-brown.
Stem: Coarse fibrous flocci, which turn brownish with age, over light skin; evenly thick.
Flesh: White; with strong smell of radish.
Habitat & distribution: From September often in large masses in lines and circles in deciduous woodland; frequent.
Poisonous: causes long-term gastric problems if eaten.
Similar species: Calocybe gambosa (118) grows in spring, is mealy, not slippery, and has a paler cap. Some species of the Cortinariales (see p. 245) are also similar: they too have slimy caps, but their stems are not floccose.

216 *Hebeloma senescens* ☠

Cap: Hemispherical when young, later convex to flat; pale clay-coloured to reddish-brown; very slippery when young, dry when old, often with dark brown blotches; the long, inrolled margin is distinctly crenate; up to 8 cm in diameter, rarely larger.
Gills: Whitish-grey when young, later ochre-brown, crowded, with floccose edge at first. *Spores:* Greyish-brown.
Stem: Usually short and with coarse, bulbous, rooting base, which turns brown with age; more rarely long and almost evenly thick, covered thickly with white flocci.
Flesh: Off-white; without scent when young, later smelling pleasantly of cocoa powder.
Habitat & distribution: Mostly in large groups from mid-September, in deciduous and coniferous woodland, mainly along forest roads and in grassy pine nurseries; frequent on chalk.

214

215

216

217 *Inocybe erubescens* ☠

Cap: First bell-shaped, later broad, with strong, blunt umbo; pale straw-coloured to hazel-brown; tearing from margin when old; turning slowly brick-red when bruised; mostly 4-6 cm rarely to 10 cm in diameter.
Gills: At first white with distinct pink hue, later olive-brown; rather crowded and with minutely floccose edge. *Spores:* Tobacco-brown.
Stem: At first white, later straw-coloured and reddening; evenly thick occasionally with distinct bulb at base.
Flesh: White, reddening; with sweet smell and unpleasant taste.
Habitat & distribution: From May to June in deciduous woodland and parks; not frequent, but locally in large numbers.
The fungal poison muscarin, which *Inocybe erubescens* contains in large measure, slows the blood circulation considerably and can be fatal. The effect of the poison can be largely neutralized by atropin, the poison of belladonna.
Similar species: Inocybe adaequata is rather similar in shape and size, but it has a dark wine-red cap from the start and a pale stem which slowly discolours brownish-lilac at its base. It occurs in moist places in deciduous and coniferous forests. Like all other brown-gilled fungi it should not be eaten (further inocybes are illustrated on p. 105).

218 *Inocybe bongardii* ☠

Cap: Inrolled when young, later bell-shaped or convex; reddish-brown and with woolly scales; 3-7 cm, rarely up to 10 cm in diameter.
Gills: Light grey-brown, can be red- or olive-brown when old; with light edge. *Spores:* Tobacco-brown.
Stem: Pale reddish-brown; rather long, pruinose at the apex and fibrous towards the base.
Flesh: Off-white, reddening slowly; with sweet, fruity smell.
Habitat & distribution: In deciduous and coniferous forests, quite frequent.
Similar species: Occasionally *Tricholoma vaccinum* (127) is very similar, but the fruity smell is absent and spores are white.

219 *Inocybe fraudans* ☠

Cap: Bell-shaped when young, soon flat with broad, blunt umbo; straw-coloured with darker fibres or small scales; later tearing from the margin; mostly 4-6 cm, seldom to 9 cm in diameter.
Gills: Whitish-grey, then watery cinnamon-brown. *Spores:* Tobacco-brown.
Stem: Light straw-coloured with pruinose apex, somewhat fibrous towards base; rather strong.
Flesh: Off-white, occasionally reddening; with very strong, sickeningly sweet smell that is reminiscent of ripe pears.
Habitat & distribution: In deciduous and coniferous forests, predominantly in moist places ; rather frequent.
Similar species: Inocybe corydalina is a little smaller, its apex is slightly scaly with a mostly dirty-green hue. It too smells sweet and fruity.

217

218

219

220 *Cortinarius orellanus* ☠ ☒

Cap: Convex to flat, occasionally with broad umbo; bright orange-brown to fox-brown; minutely scaly when young, can be bare later; does not pale on drying; 3-8 cm in diameter.
Gills: Vividly cinnamon-brown; very broad, thick and distant.
Spores: Rust-brown.
Stem: Light brassy-yellow, somewhat fibrous, cylindrical.
Flesh: Orange-yellow; emitting distinct smell of radish when cut.
Habitat & distribution: Grows almost only in warmer regions, mostly in deciduous woodland with occasional pines; rare, so should be protected.
This fungus contains the poison orellanin which damages the kidneys and is often fatal. The effect of the poison is evident only after 1-2 weeks. Because gastric problems often to not occur, and the kidney-damage is not always recognized as caused by fungal poisoning, the source of the illness often remains undiscovered for a long time. Convalescence can take more than a year and death can occur up to 6 months after the fungus is eaten.

221 *Cortinarius rubellus* ☠

Cap: Conical to bell-shaped when young, later expanded, but always with a robust, pointed umbo; vividly orange- to fox-brown and minutely scaly; up to 6 cm in diameter.
Gills: Dark cinnamon-brown; very broad, thick and distant, sinuate.
Spores: Rust-brown.
Stem: Same colour as cap; fibrous and clothed in lemon-yellow flakes; evenly thick, very long and usually deeply hidden in moss.
Flesh: Orange-brown throughout; with weak radish smell.
Habitat & distribution: In moist and boggy coniferous forests; apparently confined to the Alps, where it is frequent.
Like several related species, this fungus contains the poison orellanin; consumption causes severe kidney damage; deaths have not yet been proved, but may be possible.

222 *Cortinarius callisteus* ☠ ☒

Cap: Hemispherical when young, later convex to flat; at first bright orange-yellow and minutely scaly, somewhat darker when old; 3-6 cm in diameter.
Gills: At first orange yellow, later yellowish-brown; rather thick, moderately crowded. *Spores:* Rust-brown.
Stem: Orange-yellow and with reddish-brown scales or fibres; strong, with gradually widening, club-shaped base.
Flesh: Vividly orange-yellow, with smell of hot, oily tin.
Habitat & distribution: Singly or in small groups, in coniferous forests, mainly at higher altitudes; fairly rare and should be protected.
Due to its close relationship with the very poisonous cortinarias, this fungus should not be eaten even though there is no proof that it is poisonous.

220

221

222

223 *Cortinarius traganus* ☠

Cap: Hemispherical when young and perched button-like on thick stem, later convex, with felty, fringed margin, flat when old; at first pale amethyst-violet with silky scales, becoming paler later and discolouring to ochre; up to 12 cm in diameter.
Gills: From the start orange- to ochre-brown, later dark rust-brown; somewhat distant. *Spores:* Rust-brown.
Stem: Pale lilac, turning brown at base; below the fibrous ring-zone, which is dusted by rust-brown spores, extends a silky, blue, shimmering cover; coarse club-shaped to tuberous.
Flesh: Pale ochre-yellow, with powerful stinging smell.
Habitat & distribution: In groups in coniferous forests, mostly near bilberries; rather frequent.
When consumed, the fungus causes gastric problems; its nasty smell alone, however, is off-putting.

224 *Cortinarius camphoratus* ☠

Cap: When young, hemispherical with inrolled margin, later flat; at first beautifully amethyst-violet with silky fibres, not scaly, later growing pale, turning first ochre-grey, then light rust-brown; to 12 cm in diameter
Gills: Lovely lilac when young (distinguishing it from *C. traganus*), then watery cinnamon-brown; somewhat distant, sinuate. *Spores:* Rust-brown.
Stem: Amethyst-lilac, turning pale when old; club-shaped when young, becoming evenly thick at maturity.
Flesh: At first lilac, later ochreous; the very unpleasant smell is reminiscent of decaying potatoes.
Habitat & distribution: In coniferous forests; locally frequent.
This fungus causes gastric problems when consumed but is not often tasted due to its nasty smell.
Similar species: Lepista nuda (122), the wood blewit, has the same colours when young, but smells pleasantly sweet and never has rust-brown gills. (Other fungi with blue gills that do not discolour to rust-brown are illustrated on p. 35 and p. 67.)

225 *Cortinarius violaceus* ☠☒

Cap: Hemispherical to bell-shaped when young, soon convex or flat; at first dark metallic blue-violet and evenly minutely scaly, becoming bare and almost black when old; to 12 cm in diameter.
Gills: Dark blue-violet; rather thick, somewhat distant. *Spores:* Rust-brown; their colour forms a dust over gills when mature.
Stem: Dark violet; somewhat velvety, with fibrous ring-zone, dusted by rust-brown spores when old; thick, with coarse, club-shaped base.
Flesh: Blue-violet with strong smell of cedar wood.
Habitat & distribution: In deciduous woodland, often in fairy rings, rather rare, should be protected.
Similar species: Over the last years *Cortinarius hercynicus* has been found locally in coniferous forests with increasing frequency. Its spore dimensions differ from those of *C. violaceus*, but it is very difficult to distinguish between them.

223

224

225

226 *Cortinarius variecolor* ☠

Cap: Hemispherical when young, later convex to flat; at first a lovely violet, particularly at the margin; soon discolouring to fox-brown from the apex, the margin remaining violet for some time; slippery only when young; to 15 cm in diameter.
Gills: At first violet, later rust-brown, rather densely crowded, with a smooth or a rather crenate edge. *Spores:* Rust-brown.
Stem: Lilac-white, with silky gloss, fox-brown towards base, with fibrous ring-zone; coarsely club-shaped, but without marginated bulb.
Flesh: At first pale lilac, turning brownish later; with strong, unpleasant, dusty smell.
Habitat & distribution: In groups and fairy rings in coniferous forests; very frequent mainly at higher altitudes.
Similar species: Cortinarius nemorensis grows in deciduous woodland, mainly under beech; it is distinguished by much paler colours and smelling only weakly of dust.

227 *Cortinarius coerulescens* ☠ ☒

Cap: Hemispherical when young, later flat; at first dark blue, later discolouring to ochre, or turning pale from the apex; covered in dirty white remnants of universal veil particularly at centre; to 10 cm in diameter.
Gills: Blue-violet when young, later light rust-coloured; with serrate, light, long and blue shimmering edge. *Spores:* Rust-brown.
Stem: Deeply blue-violet; when young, overlaid closely from cap to base by the cobweb-like veil, becoming bare later; bulbous base sharply marginated, coloured pale ochre by remnants of the universal veil.
Flesh: Pale blue, deeply blue-violet at stem apex, ochreous at base; with mouldy smell, mild taste.
Habitat & distribution: Mostly in groups, in deciduous woodland, on chalk; fairly rare and should be protected.

228 *Cortinarius praestans* ☺ ☒

Cap: At first, hemispherical; thick stem supports button-like, young cap surrounded by pale violet, silky cover, later convex, flat when old; at first deep violet, soon discolouring from apex to brown-violet or wine-red; often with ochreous remains of universal veil; when old, hazel- to red-brown and striped at margin; a little slippery, to 20 cm in diameter.
Gills: Young, light or pale blue-grey, later watery rust-coloured; narrow and crowded, with crenate edge. *Spores:* Dark rust-brown.
Stem: Whitish-grey to pale lilac; coarsely bulbous; covered by vestiges of blueish-silky cover below the fibrous ring-zone.
Flesh: White; blueish in stem; very hard; without scent, mild taste.
Habitat & distribution: Often in groups or fairy rings in deciduous woodland on chalk; rare.
This fungus has the reputation of being the most tasty of the cortinarias; it is, however, rare in many areas and should be collected only where it occurs frequently.

226

227

228

229 *Cortinarius varius* ☺

Cap: Hemispherical when young, convex to almost flat when old; at first buff-orange, later becoming red-brown from the apex, yellowish-brown when old; very slimy when moist, glossy when dry; to 8 cm in diameter.
Gills: Strongly blue-violet when young, more rarely pale lilac, later watery cinnamon-brown; crowded, sinuate. *Spores:* Pale rust-brown.
Stem: White; occasionally with white woolly flocci when young, but mostly bare; with evenly round, broad, club- or onion-shaped bulbous base; with a fibrous ring-zone in the middle, stained rust-brown by spores.
Flesh: White; without scent, mild taste.
Habitat & distribution: Mostly in large groups in coniferous forests on chalk; one of the tastiest cortinarias.
Similar species: There is a whole series of slimy cortinaria species with yellow- to orange-brown cap, blue gills and white stem. With the exception of *C. delibutus* (230), they mostly have a broadly marginate, bulbous stem. Confusing them is not dangerous, as none are poisonous. The genus *Cortinarius* is the largest of all the genera of gill fungi and the most difficult to identify. In Europe alone around 600 species have been described. All cortinarias live in symbiosis with various species of trees. They have rust-brown spores, and under a microscope a coarse warty spore surface is revealed. The veil of cortinarias consists of fungal threads; in the young fungus it spans the gap between the cap's margin and the stem; later its remains often form a ring-like zone around the stem.

230 *Cortinarius delibutus* ☠

Cap: Hemispherical when young, later convex or flat; beautifully ochre- to golden-yellow, can be brownish-yellow when old; very slimy when moist; glossy when dry; to 8 cm in diameter.
Gills: At first pale lilac, later watery cinnamon-brown, somewhat distant and sinuate, with crenate edge. *Spores:* Rust-brown.
Stem: White; occasionally with shimmering violet apex; rather long, with bulbous base; closely below cap there is a fibrous ring-zone, dusted rust-brown with spores; stem is yellowish and slimy below (this distinguishes it from *C. varius*).
Flesh: White in stem apex, sometimes slightly blue; no scent, mild taste.
Habitat & distribution: Forms groups in coniferous forests and near birches; not rare.
Similar species: The slimy cortinarias have weakly sticky to very slippery stems and yellow- to greyish-brown, more rarely violet, caps. The gills are usually clay-coloured to rust-brown. Some species are very bitter. Many are similar and positive identification is in many instances only possible with the aid of a microscope.

229

230

231 *Cortinarius splendens v. meinhardii* ☠

Cap: Hemispherical when young, later convex, can be flat when old; first sulphur- to golden-yellow and slippery, later with fox-brown, umber or olive-brown blotches at the apex; up to 8 cm in diameter.
Gills: Golden-yellow when young, soon dusted by rust-brown spores; thin and very crowded. *Spores:* Dark rust-brown.
Stem: Light sulphur-yellow; with broad, sharply marginated bulbous base; covered by a yellow cobweb-like universal veil when young.
Flesh: Vibrant lemon-yellow throughout; somewhat stinging dusty scent.
Habitat & distribution: Usually only in October, often in groups in coniferous highland forests; not rare; may be poisonous.
Similar species: Cortinarius splendens grows in deciduous woodland, its cap has more olive-brown blotches, but it is otherwise hard to distinguish. It is supposed to contain the dangerous fungal poison orellanin (compare the trichlomas with yellow gills, p. 73).

232 *Cortinarius odorifer* ☺

Cap: At first convex, later flat or somewhat funnel-shaped; at the centre red-brown, often greenish or lilac towards the margin; very slimy; to 11 cm in diameter.
Gills: At first light greenish, later vividly olive-brown; crowded.
Spores: Dark rust-brown.
Stem: Yellowish-green; strong with broad, marginated bulbous base with red blotches; on the young fungus the veil stretches from margin of cap to base.
Flesh: A cut surface is vividly green yellow with a very strong smell of aniseed.
Habitat & distribution: Mostly in groups or fairy rings in coniferous forests on chalk; frequent particularly at higher altitudes.
Similar species: The cap, gills and stem of *Cortinarius orichalceus* are of similar colouration, but it has white flesh and does not smell of aniseed; it grows in coniferous and deciduous woodland on chalk, mainly in the mountains. There is a danger of confusing it with *C. splendens v. meinhardii* (231), which is suspected of being poisonous.

233 *Cortinarius scaurus* ☠

Cap: Convex when young, later flat, often with broad umbo, very slippery; dark olive-brown; with brown water stains at the margin when old; rather small, mostly 3-5 cm in diameter.
Gills: Blue to olive-green when young, sometimes somewhat lilac; more greyish- brown when old; thin, crowded, with serrate edge.
Spores: Rust-brown.
Stem: Light olive-green; covered by cobweb-like fibrous veil from cap margin to bulbous base when young; rather slender, bulbous base very broad and blunt.
Flesh: Brownish in the cap, yellowish-green in stem, though can be rather blue at the top; sometimes discolouring weakly purple when bruised.
Habitat & distribution: In boggy coniferous forests and boggy pine forests of higher altitudes, mainly in Alpine foot hills; very rare.

231

232

233

234 *Cortinarius cephalixus* ☠ ☒

Cap: Convex when young, later flat; weakly slippery; light ochre-brown, slightly grainy, sometimes with greenish-yellow hues particularly towards the margin; to 10 cm in diameter.
Gills: Clay-coloured, at first pale, later deepening; rather crowded, sinuate. *Spores:* Rust-brown.
Stem: With several dirty olive belts below the fibrous ring-zone; coarse, bulbous.
Flesh: White; mild taste, smell of cut grass.
Habitat & distribution: In deciduous woodland, mainly under beech, on chalk; fairly rare.
Similar species: The cap of *Cortinarius cliduchus* is more buff-ochre, also slightly grainy and weakly slippery; the stem is clothed in pure yellow flakes. Both fungi grow in deciduous woodland and are often so similar as to be hardly distinguishable.

235 *Cortinarius percomis* ☠

Cap: Hemispherical when young, later convex; moist, slippery; at first ochre- to lemon-yellow at the margin, later becoming buff-coloured to fox-brown from the apex; to 7 cm in diameter.
Gills: Vividly lemon-yellow when young, yellowish-brown when old; crowded, sinuate or slightly decurrent. *Spores:* Rust-brown.
Stem: Bright lemon-yellow, rather long and slender, with a fibrous ring-zone, dusted rust-brown by spores, blotchy brown below; base not marginated or bulbous, but weakly club-shaped.
Flesh: Vividly lemon-yellow, with strong smell of marjoram.
Habitat & distribution: In coniferous forests, on chalk, mainly at higher altitudes, locally frequent.
Similar species: Cortinarius splendens (231) and some other cortinarias have rather similar colouration, however, they often have a marginated bulbous base and never smell of marjoram.

236 *Cortinarius rufoolivaceus* ☠ ☒

Cap: Convex when young, later flat, moist and slippery; at first pale purplish-lilac, later discolouring to wine-red from apex; up to 10 cm in diameter.
Gills: Yellowish-green when young, later dirty rust- to cinnamon-brown; crowded, sinuate. *Spores:* Dark rust-brown.
Stem: Off-white to beautifully violet, can be wine-red at bulb; rather strong with a broadly marginated bulb and at the base; covered at immaturity by a universal veil that spans from cap margin to base.
Flesh: Pale violet, can be yellowish in the cap, more rarely yellowish-green; without scent, occasionally rather bitter taste.
Habitat & distribution: Usually in moist areas in deciduous woodland on chalky soil, also under silver firs; fairly rare and should be protected.

234

235

236

237 *Cortinarius bolaris* ☠

Cap: Broadly bell-shaped when young, later convex, often contorted; pale clay-coloured skin covered densely by small carmine-red scales, sometimes uniformly red; to 8 cm in diameter.
Gills: Pale clay-coloured, later coffee- to rust-brown; narrow and not crowded, with minutely floccose edge. *Spores:* Cinnamon-brown.
Stem: Concolorous with cap, apex with distinct pale clay colour; clothed in small, red, fibrous scales below.
Flesh: White; turning slightly yellow when bruised; with weak, dusty scent, mild taste.
Habitat: Below beech, mainly in moist areas; fairly rare.

238 *Cortinarius fluryi* ☠

Cap: Hemispherical when young, later convex, often flat, with down-turned margin; dark chestnut-brown and rather grainy; often covered by white, fibrous remnants of the veil at the rim; a little slippery when immature; up to 9 cm in diameter.
Gills: At first dirty off-white, later deep clay-brown; rather broad, sinuate, a little distant. *Spores:* Dark rust-brown.
Stem: With a fibrous ring-zone; covered in white woolly scales below; weakly club-shaped at base.
Flesh: White; with sweet scent, which becomes unpleasantly mouldy later.
Habitat & distribution: Often in clusters, in deciduous forests under beech; fairly rare.

239 *Cortinarius collinitus* ☠

Cap: Bell-shaped when young, later broadly domed, often with flat, indistinct umbo; matt, rust-brown, more rarely orange-brown; very slimy, not grooved; up to 10 cm in diameter.
Gills: At first clay-coloured, soon light rust-brown, slightly sinuate, often adnate when old. *Spores:* Yellow-brown.
Stem: Rather long, evenly thick and often somewhat attenuate at the base; below the fibrous ring-zone covered in bluish-white to vividly blue-violet sticky slime, often tearing when old, therefore striped.
Flesh: Off-white; watery with mild taste, without scent.
Habitat & distribution: In groups in coniferous forests, mostly near spruce; frequent; very changeable.

240 *Cortinarius glaucopus* ☠

Cap: Hemispherical when young, soon expanded, with wavy contorted margin; fox-brown, often lighter olive-green towards margin; very fibrous; moist, slippery; up to 12 cm in diameter.
Gills: First blue-lilac, later more clay-coloured, crowded, shallow and sinuate. *Spores:* Rust-brown.
Stem: Initially glossy and blue, later brassy-brown; usually short and strong, with a small, marginate, distinct bulb at the base.
Flesh: Yellowish-white in cap, in stem vividly blue, no scent, mild.
Habitat & distribution: Often numerous, forming dense, wide rows; in conifer forests; frequent.

237
left
238
right
239
240

241 *Cortinarius hinnuleus* ☠ Fawn Cortinarius

Cap: First broadly bell-shaped, later almost flat and often with a distinct, broad umbo; dark yellowish-brown when moist, dirty ochre when dry, often with dark blotches; rather thick flesh; to 8 cm in diameter.
Gills: Rust-brown; very broad, deeply sinuate, noticeably distant.
Spores: Cinnamon-brown.
Stem: Dirty yellow- to ochre-brown; strong, base usually club-shaped; with irregular, dirty-white flakes or belts towards base.
Flesh: Brownish, watery-marbled; typically with an earthy smell.
Habitat: Mostly in groups, in deciduous woodland, rather frequent.

242 *Cortinarius armillatus* ☠☒

Red-banded Cortinarius

Cap: At first bell-shaped, later flattening out; vividly fox- to rust-brown, becoming slightly paler with age, with small fibrous scales; to 15 cm in diameter.
Gills: Dark rust-brown, very broad and distant, shallowly sinuate.
Spores: Rust-brown.
Stem: Flesh-brown, with several red, floccose belts below the fibrous ring-zone; evenly thick to coarsely club-shaped.
Flesh: Brownish and marbled, without scent, mild taste.
Habitat & distribution: Often in large groups under scattered birches and in coniferous forests, prefers moist spots; fairly rare and should be protected.
Similar species: Cortinarius paragaudis is somewhat smaller and the apex of its cap not as strongly rust-brown. The lower part if its fairly long stalk has several red-brown, floccose zones. This relatively rare fungus grows near birch, and also in mountain forests.

243 *Cortinarius brunneus* ☠

Cap: Bell-shaped when young, later expanded with low, blunt umbo; dark brown when moist, light reddish to buff when dry, margin silky; to 8 cm in diameter.
Gills: Dark brown, very broad, thick and striped, distant. *Spores:* Rust-brown.
Stem: Dark brown, usually with a club-shaped base and fibrous, soon vanishing, ring-zone; a white membranous zone below discolours to pale grey-brown with age.
Flesh: Dark brown, marbled; with earthy smell, mild taste.
Habitat & distribution: Mostly in groups in moist conifer forests, among moss, not rare.
Similar species: Cortinarius glandicolor is smaller and grows also in moist places of coniferous forests. When moist, the fungus is evenly umber-brown, and paler when dry; stem zonation is usually absent.

241

242

243

244 *Cortinarius balaustinus* ☠ ☒

Cap: Hemispherical when young, later flattening and often irregularly contorted; when moist, vividly rust-to fox-brown, becoming striped when dry, then light reddish-ochre; to 9 cm in diameter.
Gills: Vividly rust-coloured; thick, broad and rather distant, often interconnected, sinuate. *Spores:* Rust-brown.
Stem: Light rust-brown; slender, weakly fibrous with coarsely club-shaped and somewhat attenuated base, rooting in the soil.
Flesh: Rust-brown, marbled throughout; without scent, mild taste.
Habitat & distribution: Mostly in small groups, in deciduous woodland; rare, should be protected.
Similar species: Cortinarius subbalaustinus looks almost the same, but grows only under birches. Both species can be distinguished immediately when examined under a microscope as *C. balaustinus* has round spores, *C. subbalaustinus* elliptical ones. The latter species is very rare and has been found only a few times in Europe.

245 *Cortinarius bulliardii* ☠

Cap: Bell-shaped when young, red-brown and with fibrous scales, later broadly cone-shaped, with indistinct, blunt umbo; when moist, dark chestnut-brown, dirty buff when dry; to 7 cm in diameter.
Gills: First pale lilac, soon watery cinnamon-brown; rather broad and only moderately crowded. *Spores:* Rust-brown.
Stem: Occasionally pale lilac at apex when immature, otherwise whitish, the lower half covered by vivid red fibres; short, with club-shaped base.
Flesh: Dirty-white, watery lilac-brown at stem apex; weakly bitter taste.
Habitat & distribution: Mostly in small groups in deciduous woodland under beech; fairly rare.
Similar species: Cortinarius colus is very much smaller and has a light brown stem the base of which is also overlaid with red fibres. This fungus is at most 2 cm in diameter and found in moist conifer forests, but is quite rare.

246 *Cortinarius laniger*

Cap: Hemispherical when young, later convex to flat; light red-brown, turning slightly paler, initially with overlay of silky fibres; to 10 cm in diameter.
Gills: Vividly red-brown; thick, distant. *Spores:* Rust-brown.
Stem: White, occasionally slightly lilac at the apex when young, usually with two ring-like belts; coarsely club- to bulb-shaped.
Flesh: Light brown, marbled; mild taste.
Habitat & distribution: In groups or rows, in deciduous and coniferous forests; rather frequent at higher altitudes.
Similar species: Cortinarius cinamoviolaceus also grows in coniferous mountain forests; it is far more rare and can be distinguished by its deep lilac stem.

244
245
246

247 *Paxillus involutus* ☠ Brown Roll-rim

Cap: Flat when young, later convex or funnel-shaped; with felted, often notched and long inrolled rim, apex bare; dirty ochre to red-brown; slippery when moist, glossy when dry; to 15 cm in diameter.
Gills: Wood-yellow, turning dark red-brown when bruised; narrow and crowded, often forked, decurrent, can be detached from flesh of cap.
Spores: Light rust-brown.
Stem: Same colour as cap, developing brown blotches when bruised; rather slender, with firm flesh.
Flesh: Light wood-yellow, with pleasant smell.
Habitat & distribution: In coniferous forests and fens; on the forest floor or on stumps; very frequent.
Paxillus involutus is a particularly dangerous poisonous fungus because it is harmless if eaten singly and well cooked. Eaten raw, or insufficiently cooked, it causes severe or even fatal poisonings. After repeated consumption it can lead to sudden poisonings even if prepared correctly; even with an interval of years between eating the fungus, several people have been fatally poisoned. This fungus contains an as yet unknown agent which accumulates in the blood and triggers the formation of antibodies. If, after repeated intake a critical threshold is surpassed, a poisoning that appears like leukaemia is observed. Do not taste this fungus, or use it for cooking.

248 *Paxillus filamentosus* ☠

Cap: Highly resembles *P. involutus* in colour and form, but is smaller and sometimes almost attached to stalk at the side (excentric), more funnel-shaped and contorted.
Gills: As in *P. involutus*, but not forked and turning only weakly blotchy.
Spores: Rust-brown.
Stem & Flesh: As in *P. involutus*.
Habitat & distribution: Often in larger groups or fairy rings, only below alders, mostly in damp localities; not frequent.
Do not consume as effects similar to those in *P. involutus* are possible.

249 *Paxillus atrotomentosus* ☠ Dark Downy Paxillus

Cap: Flat when young, later funnel-shaped, mostly stalked at the side (excentric), with long, inrolled margin; fleshy; dark brown and velvety, becoming bare and a little paler when old; up to 15 cm in diameter.
Gills: Light wood-yellow, not blotchy when bruised; narrow and very crowded, decurrent. *Spores:* Rust-brown.
Stem: Dark brown and velvety; very short, the base rooting a little.
Flesh: Light wood-yellow; juicy, somewhat bitter taste.
Habitat & distribution: Only on conifer stumps, mostly in damp and shady localities; rather frequent.

247

248

249

250 *Gomphidius rutilus* ☺

Cap: Convex when young, with inrolled margin, flattening out later; at first copper-brown, then a little paler; very slimy when moist, smooth and glossy when dry; very fleshy; to 8 cm in diameter.
Gills: Purple-brown when young, soon with dirty olive-brown hue; very thick, distant, often forked and decurrent. *Spores:* Olive-black.
Stem: Same colour as the cap; long and slender, with firm flesh.
Flesh: Orange-yellow, turning carmine red after a while when bruised; no scent, mild taste.
Habitat & distribution: Only under pines; not rare.
Similar species: Closely related species from the family Gomphidiaceae with white to pale grey gills are *Gomphidius roseus* (111) and *G. glutinosus* (112).

251 *Gomphidius helveticus* ☠ ☒

Cap: Convex when young, flatter when old; beautifully orange with small fibrous scales, bare when old, seldom slightly sticky, very fleshy; to 8 cm in diameter.
Gills: Orange-brown due to olive-black spores; thick distant, decurrent. *Spores:* Olive-black.
Stem: Orange-brown; evenly thick, a little floccose at apex.
Flesh: Orange-yellow to brown, turning slowly carmine red when bruised; mild taste.
Habitat & distribution: Only under pines and stone pines; rare, should be protected.

252 *Lacrymaria lacrymabunda* ☠

Cap: Convex when young, later flat and often with broad umbo; at first felted with woolly scales over a yellow-brown pellicle; with a fibrous veil spanning from the rim of the cap to the stem, later becoming bare, pale when drying out; mostly 3-6 cm, occasionally to 20 cm in diameter.
Gills: First brownish, soon blackish-purple; the light edge appears floccose due to water droplets so minute that they can only be seen under a microscope. *Spores:* Dark purplish-brown, almost black.
Stem: Pale brownish, with fibrous scales and a snake-like pattern.
Flesh: Light clay-brown; mild taste, no scent.
Habitat & distribution: At waysides, between broken stones, on fields, in gardens, on loose bark; frequent and occasionally in large numbers.
Similar species: *Lacrymaria lacrymabunda* belongs to a group of gill fungi which contains more than 100 species. Most of these are in the genus *Psathyrella* (brittle caps). They are recognized by their almost black spores and a very brittle cap. This group of fungi is problematic as the family can only be identified using a microscope.

250

251

252

253 *Russula xyanoxantha* ☺ Charcoal Burner

Cap: Convex when young, soon expanded, funnel-shaped when old; colouration very variable, mostly blue-violet with green spots, lighter at the centre and sometimes paling to ochre, occasionally entirely green or dark steel-blue; slippery when moist; up to 12 cm in diameter.
Gills: Pure white; thin, crowded, fairly soft, not breaking on bending, adnate, somewhat decurrent when old. *Spores:* Pure white.
Stem: Pure white, occasionally with a hint of the cap's colour when young; strong, evenly thick or slightly attenuated.
Flesh: White; brittle; without scent, with mild, nutty taste.
Habitat & distribution: From June mainly in deciduous woodlands and in mixed forests; very frequent.
Use: Suitable for many kinds of preparation; flesh not as hard as that of most other edible russulas.
Similar species: The cap of the grey-green russula (*Russula grisea*) is more blue-grey but also has violet or green hues and light cream gills. This fungus also grows in mixed forests, particularly under beech, and more rarely in coniferous forests.

254 *Russula aeruginea* ☠ Grass-green Russula

Cap: Flat when young, soon funnel-shaped and weakly striped; somewhat sticky and shiny; pale green or light grey-green, more rarely also olive-green; mostly 5-8 cm, rarely up to 12 cm in diameter.
Gills: Pale cream when young, later light butter-yellow; crowded, frequently forked at the place of attachment, tensile and do not break when stroked. *Spores:* Dark cream.
Stem: White, occasionally with rust-coloured spots at the base; evenly thick, often rather short with longitudinal furrows.
Flesh: White; brittle, without scent, gills rather pungent, taste otherwise mild.
Habitat & distribution: Only under birch, mostly in pine forests with scattered birch stands; not rare.

255 *Russula vesca* ☺ Bared Teeth Russula

Cap: Hemispherical when young, soon flat, can be funnel-shaped when old; margin never striped but a 2 mm wide zone remains white because the cap's epidermis is too short; somewhat sticky when moist, without lustre when dry; a fleshy lilac to purple when young, later often with light rust-brown spots; up to 8 cm in diameter.
Gills: White, with rusty spots when old; narrow, crowded, adnate, projecting from the margin; rather soft. *Spores:* White.
Stem: White, somewhat bulbous or thick, attenuate at the base and often with rusty spots.
Flesh: White, often with rusty or honey-yellow spots; rather firm, without scent, with mild taste.
Habitat & distribution: From June in deciduous and coniferous forests; very frequent.
Use: One of the best tasting russulas, but the flesh is hard and has little volume.

253

254

255

256 *Russula turci* ☺

Cap: Flat when young, soon somewhat funnel-shaped; dark amethyst-violet to brownish-pink, margin paler; noticeably matt and pruinose; up to 8 cm in diameter.
Gills: Cream to light ochre, rather crowded, connected at the base by cross veins. *Spores:* Ochre.
Stem: White, evenly thick.
Flesh: White; the base of the stem has a distinct smell of iodine.
Habitat & distribution: Under pines and spruces, on sandy soil and clay; rather frequent.
Similar species: The rare *Russula azurea* also has a strongly pruinose, blackish-purple cap and grows beneath spruces. The *Russula amethystina* can hardly be distinguished from *R. turci*. Its blue- to reddish-violet cap occasionally has pale patches and also a smell of iodine in the stem base; it is frequent in coniferous mountain forests, mostly under silver firs.

257 *Russula olivacea* ☺

Cap: Convex when young, soon flat, not funnel-shaped; entirely yellowish-olive when young, without lustre and dull wine-red to rusty-brown often with a dirty-olive slightly corrugated margin; up to 15 cm in diameter.
Gills: Cream, deep ochre when old, crowded and rather brittle.
Spores: Egg-yellow.
Stem: Pale pink, apex lightly covered in tufts; strong, evenly thick, with firm flesh.
Flesh: White; rather hard and firm, without scent, mild taste.
Habitat & distribution: Mostly in groups, from June in deciduous and coniferous forests, mainly under spruce and beech; not rare.
Similar species: Russula viscida (leather stem russula) is in size and habitat deceptively similar to *R. olivacea*; the surface of its cap is bright purple- to blood-red and shiny, the margin pales sometimes to light ochre. Its coarse stem is never reddish, but its base turns leather-yellow when old; the flesh is rather pungent. *R. viscida* grows in coniferous mountain forests.

258 *Russula integra* ☺

Cap: Convex when young, soon funnel-shaped; usually reddish-purple with an almost black centre when young; middle later light brown, but frequently also flesh- to chocolate-brown; usually somewhat slippery and shiny; with weakly striped margin when old; up to 10 cm in diameter.
Gills: At first cream, deep ochre-yellow when old; often branching at the base and crumbling easily if touched. *Spores:* Dark ochre.
Stem: Always pure white, occasionally a little brown at the base; rather long, often obese.
Flesh: White; noticeably hard, firm; mild taste, weak fruity scent.
Habitat & distribution: In coniferous and deciduous forests, beneath spruce and fir, very frequent at greater altitudes.
Similar species: Russula adulterina has very acrid flesh and is distinguishable only by taste. It grows in a similar habitat, but is far more rare.

256

257

258

259 *Russula foetens* ☠ Stinking Russula

Cap: Hemispherical and very slimy when young, later convex, can be flat or somewhat funnel-shaped when old, rim comb-like; dingy honey-yellow to ochre-brown; up to 15 cm in diameter.
Gills: Pale cream; often with water droplets on the edge when young, rather broad and crowded. *Spores:* Pale cream.
Stem: White or blotchy yellowish-brown; strong.
Flesh: With a strong, nasty acrid smell, when old has a fishy smell, rather acrid taste.
Habitat & distribution: In deciduous and in coniferous forests; fairly frequent.

260 *Russula ochroleuca* ☠ Common Yellow Russula

Cap: Flat when young, soon expanded and funnel-shaped; light lemon-yellow to dirty olive-ochre; moist, sticky; up to 10 cm in diameter.
Gills: Pure white, never with cream or yellowish hues even when old; crowded and breaking easily. *Spores:* Pale cream.
Stem: White, coloured as the cap at its base when young, slightly greying when old; evenly thick.
Flesh: White, with very weak fruity scent, mild to rather hot taste.
Habitat & distribution: One of the most common russulas in deciduous and in coniferous forests; very frequent.
Similar species: Russula claroflava, the yellow swamp russula. has a bright chrome-yellow cap and completely mild flesh that turns grey on ageing; it grows under birches in swamps.

261 *Russula fellea* ☠ Geranium-scented Russula

Cap: Hemispherical when young, later flat to slightly funnel-shaped, with broad comb-like margin when old; light straw-coloured to ochre; up to 8 cm in diameter.
Gills: Pale cream from the start; crowded, mostly adnate. *Spores:* Pale cream.
Stem: Pale cream; evenly thick.
Flesh: Pale yellowish; distinct sweet, fruity smell, acrid taste.
Habitat & distribution: In great numbers in deciduous forests, often with *R. ochroleuca* (260); frequent.

262 *Russula illota* ☠

Cap: Spherical when young, later broadly convex, can be flat when old; dirty ochre-coloured; covered with grey-violet slime, with coarse comb-like stripes at the margin; to 15 cm in diameter.
Gills: Cream; close together; with dark spots and dashes along the edge; giving off a bitter almond smell when rubbed. *Spores:* Pale cream.
Stem: Dingy white, becoming blotchy with brown spots with age.
Flesh: With smell of bitter almonds.
Habitat & distribution: In deciduous and coniferous forests, mainly on chalk; rather frequent.
Similar species: Russula laurocerasi, not yet technically distinguished from *R. illota*. It smells of bitter almonds, but the edge of its gills lacks punctuation and the colour of its cap is more like that of *R. foetens*. The rubbed gills smell very unpleasant.

259

left
260
right
261

262

263 *Russula mustelina* ☺

Cap: Hemispherical when young, later convex to flat or with a depression at the centre; yellowish-brown; slippery when young; soon without lustre and drying out; occasionally with a bloom on the margin, veins running from the apex to the rim of the cap and fairly similar to a Penny-bun (1); up to 16 cm in diameter.
Gills: Pale cream, later yellowish with an ochre reflex, with brownish blotches when old; rather close together, sinuate near stem.
Spores: Cream.
Stem: White when young, soon marbled with brownish hue; somewhat tuberous and obese or immediately thick, rather firm and compact.
Flesh: White, turning slightly brown when old; rather hard and firm, mild taste, smelling unpleasantly fishy after prolonged storage.
Habitat & distribution: Only in mountains on chalkless soil; frequent in the central Alps.

264 *Russula aurea* ☺

Cap: Almost spherical when young, later becoming flat and irregularly convex to funnel-shaped; stained bright lemon- to golden-yellow deep into cap flesh, with large, bright-orange to cadmium-red spots above; more rarely uniformly yellow or red; slippery and shiny, weakly notched at the rim when old, up to 8 cm in diameter.
Gills: Pale yellow, can be bright golden yellow when old; the edge is a strong chrome-yellow from the start; very brittle and often interconnected at the base by cross-veins.
Stem: White, often suffused with golden-yellow, with longitudinal stripes, somewhat club-shaped or attenuate at the base.
Flesh: White; rather soft, mild taste, without scent. *Spores:* Egg-yellow.
Habitat & distribution: Mostly singly in deciduous woodland and in coniferous forests; not frequent.
Use: This fungus is suitable for all recipes and often considered to be the most palatable russula.
Similar species: Russula maculata also has a bright red cap which pales to ochre or lemon-yellow; it gills are yellow, orange-ochre when old; its flesh tastes mild at first, but becomes rather acrid with prolonged chewing. This fungus is inedible.

265 *Russula decolorans* ☺

Cap: Convex, with depressed centre when old; beautifully orange to brick-red or apple-coloured; slightly slippery when young; up to 10 cm in diameter.
Gills: Pale cream when young, later butter-yellow, greying with age.
Flesh: White, turning grey when old; mild taste. *Spores:* Pale ochre.
Habitat & distribution: In coniferous forests with blueberries; locally in large groups.
Similar species: Pale forms of *Russula paludosa*, which often grow in the same habitat; they can be distinguished by their more bell-shaped cap; their flesh does not turn grey.

263

264

265

266 *Russula mairei* ☠ Beechwood Sickener

Cap: Convex when young, soon irregularly contorted to weakly funnel-shaped, notched at the margin when old; pink to cinnabar-red, frequently turning pale in blotches; sticky and shiny when moist; up to 6 cm in diameter.
Gills: White; standing very close together, adnate to the stem.
Spores: White.
Stem: White, never with shades of red; evenly thick or somewhat obese, very brittle.
Flesh: White; with a pleasant, acidic scent reminiscent of unripe apples, very hot taste.
Habitat & distribution: Mostly in groups in deciduous woodland under beeches; very frequent. The beechwood sickener is regarded as weakly poisonous as eating it causes stomach upsets and abdominal pains.
Similar species: The true 'sickener' (*Russula emetica f. sylvestris*) usually has a deeply cherry-red cap, but is otherwise similar to the beechwood sickener; it is also very hot and inedible. It is found predominantly in coniferous forests frequently among moss in moist places, but also in deciduous woodland, where it is almost impossible to distinguish from *R. mairei*.

267 *Russula cavipes* ☠

Cap: Convex when young, soon flat or somewhat funnel-shaped; a dingy lilac and frequently with olive-green blotches, almost black at the centre, blue-violet at the margin; up to 6 cm in diameter.
Gills: White; close together and very brittle. *Spores:* White.
Stem: White, without red hues; somewhat distended and very brittle.
Flesh: White; with an acidic taste of unripe fruits, very hot taste.
Habitat & distribution: In deciduous and coniferous forests; rather frequent; eating the fungus causes stomach and abdominal pains.

268 *Russula paludosa* ☺

Cap: Hemispherical when young, soon broadly bell-shaped, somewhat notched at the margin when old; almost always with a small depression at the apex; a little sticky and shiny when moist; coloured like a red-cheeked apple, from golden-yellow to bright blood-red and frequently with two colours, occasionally almost black at the centre, can be yellow at the rim or apex; up to 10 cm in diameter.
Gills: Cream when young, later butter-yellow; rather close together; splintering slightly if brushed. *Spores:* Pale ochre.
Stem: Usually flushed pale pink, more rarely white; evenly thick, noticeably long, with firm flesh, with visible veins.
Flesh: White, without scent, mild taste.
Habitat & distribution: In groups in coniferous forests, mostly under pines and together with blueberries; rather frequent.
Similar species: Russula badia (the cedar russula) is somewhat smaller; its cap, which is a deeper blood-red, has a somewhat funnel-shaped depression at the centre. *R. badia* can be distinguished as its flesh has an acrid, hot scent of cedar wood.

266

267

268

269 *Russula xerampelina* ☺

Cap: Convex when young, soon flat; when growing in coniferous forests mostly dark wine- to carmine-red, with black apex; by contrast, forms in deciduous woodlands are pale flesh-pink, yellowish or dirty olive; yellowish-green or green below trembling poplar and birch, frequently of more than one colour; initially slippery, but soon matt and without lustre; mostly 5-8 cm, rarely up to 12 cm in diameter.
Gills: Pale cream, turning lightly brown when bruised, rather close.
Spores: Cream.
Stem: In forms with a red cap, stem is the same colour, otherwise white, turning yellow or brown when bruised; often wrinkled longitudinally.
Flesh: White; initially without scent, but with strong herring smell when dry or old; mild taste.
Habitat & distribution: Singly or in groups in deciduous or coniferous forests; frequent.

270 *Russula rosea* ☠

Cap: Convex when young, later flat; matt, without lustre; mostly bright cinnabar- to carmine-red, often with yellow spots, rarely entirely yellowish-white; very hard; up to 10 cm in diameter.
Gills: Pale straw-yellow, very brittle, occasionally with a red edge at the rim of the cap. *Spores:* Pale cream.
Stem: Mostly flushed carmine, but also pure white; evenly thick, very hard and firm.
Flesh: White; very hard, tasting bitter, like pencil wood.
Habitat & distribution: In coniferous forests or near beech trees; rather frequent.
Similar species: The rare *Russula pseudointegra* (the ochre leaved cinnabar russula) of deciduous forests is distinguished by its quite hot tasting flesh. Red-stemmed forms of R. *rosea* could also be confused with *R. xerampelina*, but the latter has soft flesh and no woody flavour.

271 *Russula rhodopoda* ☠☒

Cap: Hemispherical when young, later bell-shaped to flat with long, upturned margin; bright purple-red, with an almost black centre, occasionally with small yellowish spots; mostly very glossy; up to 12 cm in diameter.
Gills: Initially pale cream, then butter-yellow; close together.
Spores: Cream.
Stem: White, flushed beautifully with red, with a mealy surface particularly at the base, later with yellow spots; evenly thick, club-shaped or with an obese middle.
Flesh: White, rather firm, with very hot taste and a weak, fruity smell.
Habitat & distribution: Often in large groups in acid coniferous forests, mostly in higher altitudes; rather rare.
Similar species: Russula persicina, the peach-coloured russula, is distinguished by its matt, rough cap, only slightly red stem and sweet smell. It is also possible to confuse *R.rhodopoda* with *R. sardonia* (274), the lemon-leaved russula.

269

270

271

272 *Russula laricina* ☠

Cap: Convex with depressed centre; light flesh-brown, olive at the centre, can have pink or purple, rarely yellow tones; slippery when moist, with rough marginal grooves separated by rough bumps when old; up to 6 cm in diameter.
Gills: Cream when young, later deep orange-ochre; thick and wide, rather distant, very brittle. *Spores:* Deep egg-yellow.
Stem: White, never red; with attenuated base; breaking off easily.
Flesh: White, some grey discolouration when old; very brittle; with unpleasant fishy smell, mild taste.
Habitat & distribution: In coniferous highland forests beneath larches.

273 *Russula puellaris* ☠

Cap: Convex when young, soon flat, with rough, comb-like ridges; flesh-coloured to violet-purple, almost black at the somewhat depressed centre, transparent and yellow when old; slippery and shiny for most of life, very brittle; 3-5 cm in diameter.
Gills: Watery cream-coloured when young, later ochre-yellow; thick and distant, very brittle and soft. *Spores:* Light cream.
Stem: White, later discolouring yellow; somewhat obese, hollow, very brittle.
Flesh: White, slowly discolouring yellow; with an unpleasant smell reminiscent of cod-liver oil, mild taste.
Habitat & distribution: Mostly in coniferous forests; rather frequent.

274 *Russula sardonia* ☠ Changeable Russula

Cap: Bell-shaped, later flat to funnel-shaped, usually with a raised centre; dark violet to purple, centre very dark, sometimes discolouring to olive; somewhat sticky when moist; up to 12 cm in diameter.
Gills: Beautifully lemon-yellow when young with drops of water along the edge, later light ochre; very brittle. *Spores:* Cream.
Stem: Usually flushed with purple, with a downy surface layer.
Flesh: Pale yellow; hard and firm, with acidic, fruity smell, very hot taste.
Habitat & distribution: In coniferous forests on acid soil, mostly under pines; locally common.
Eating this mushroom causes stomach upsets and abdominal pains.

275 *Russula queletii* ☠ Gooseberry Russula

Cap: Hemispherical when young, later convex to flat and often with a small umbo; dingy wine-red, usually becoming blotchy and paling to olive; bare and slippery when moist, weakly striped when old; mostly 5-6 cm, rarely up to 10 cm in diameter.
Gills: Almost white; close together and very brittle. *Spores:* Cream.
Stem: On top of a pale yellow background a dingy wine-red like that of the cap; evenly thick.
Flesh: White, with a fruity smell reminiscent of gooseberries, very hot taste.
Habitat & distribution: Mostly in groups, predominantly in forests of spruce among litter of shed needles and moss; frequent.
Eating this mushroom causes stomach upsets and abdominal pains.

272

left
273

right
274

275

276 *Russula delica* ☠ Milk-white Russula

Cap: Low, convex, with inrolled margin when young, later funnel-shaped; dirty white when young and soon with light to dark brown spots; often lifts up soil and needle litter; up to 15 cm in diameter.
Gills: White, with a blue sheen; rather broad and distant, somewhat decurrent; often with drops of water at the edge. *Spores:* White.
Stem: White, when old blotchy and slightly ochreous; very short.
Flesh: White, hard, with unpleasant fish-oil smell.
Habitat & distribution: In deciduous and in coniferous forests, mostly on chalky soil; frequent.
Similar species: Russula chloroides differs only by its narrower gills which stand closer together; it grows in the same habitat, but at greater altitudes.

277 *Russula nigricans* ☠ Blackening Russula

Cap: Flat with inrolled margin, funnel-shaped when old; whitish-grey when young, soon dark greyish-brown and black when old; up to 15 cm in diameter.
Gills: Light straw-coloured; thick and distant, very brittle; edge blackening from the margin when old. *Spores:* White.
Stem: White at first, turning black from the base when old; rather short and thick.
Flesh: White, when bruised flushing with red at first and turning black later; very hard, mild taste, without scent.
Habitat & distribution: In coniferous forests; very frequent.
Similar species: The gills of *Russula albonigra* are closer together, its flesh is rather hot and turns black when old, but never red. The cap of *Russula densifolia* is lighter grey-brown, almost white when young, its gills are close together and its flesh turns at first reddish, then black.

278 *Lactarius vellereus* ☠

Cap: Funnel-shaped with long, inrolled margin; pure white and minutely silky and woolly, with light brown blotches when old; mostly 10-17 cm, rarely up to 30 cm in diameter.
Gills: Light cream, somewhat blotchy when old; narrow, thick and distant, often forked at the stem. *Spores:* White.
Stem: White; very short and thick.
Flesh: Hard and firm, burns extremely hot on the tongue, with a white milk sap which is mild if eaten without flesh.
Habitat & distribution: In groups in deciduous forests, more rarely also in coniferous forests, very frequent everywhere.
Similar species: The peppery milk cap *Lactarius piperatus* has milk which discolours greyish-green on drying and *Lactarius glaucescens* has milk which dries greenish; both grow in similar localities. The gills of both species are close together; they have a smooth rather than silky, woolly cap. All lactarias with a white cap and hot milk cause gastric problems when eaten.

276

277

278

279 *Lactarius scrobiculatus* ☠

Cap: Hemispherical with umbilicated middle when young, soon broadly funnel-shaped with long inrolled margin; straw-coloured to pale lemon-yellow; with circular zones of flat, shaggy, fibrous scales; at first shaggy and fibrous towards the margin, becoming bare later; very slippery when young; mostly 8-15 cm, rarely up to 24 cm in diameter.
Gills: Cream-white, becoming blotchy brown when old; narrow, thick and rather close together, adnate and sometimes forked. *Spores:* Light ochre.
Stem: Lemon-yellow like the cap and minutely downy, with dark, water-stained pits; very short and thick.
Flesh: White, rather hard with white, very hot milk sap which, after 10 seconds of exposure to air, turns a lovely sulphur yellow.
Habitat & distribution: Occasionally in large masses in coniferous forests, mostly under spruce; very frequent mainly in mountainous areas and in northern Europe.
This mushroom cannot be eaten fresh. In eastern Europe it is, like many other hot milk caps, conserved in large numbers by being fermented in lactic acid and tinned.
Similar species: There are still two other closely related but exceedingly rare milk caps with a fibrous, shaggy cap. They have white milk which quickly discolours yellow. *Lactarius citriolens* has an ochre-white cap, circular fibrous shaggy zones, and an aromatic scent reminiscent of lemon peel. *Lactarius resimus* is not zonated and only weakly shaggy; it is pure white and discolours yellow when bruised. It grows in the birch forests of northern Europe (particularly Scandinavia) and is rare elsewhere.

280 *Lactarius repraesentaneus* ☠ ☒

Cap: Flat when young, hardly funnel-shaped even when old; light straw-yellow; zonated by shaggy tufts more weakly circular than *Lactarius scrobiculatus* (279); margin long inrolled and very shaggy; up to 15 cm in diameter.
Gills: Creamy-white, densely packed. *Spores:* Cream-yellow.
Stem: Light straw- to lemon-yellow; evenly thick or a little obese and about as long as the cap is wide, weakly tufted at the apex, with dark, water-stained pits, becoming hollow with age.
Flesh: Yellowish-white; hard and firm, with a spicy scent; it exudes a white milk sap which is mild or slightly bitter and sometimes assumes a violet hue immediately, but often very slowly and sometimes only after several days.
Habitat & distribution: In deciduous and in coniferous forests, mostly below spruce or birch, on chalk-free soil, mainly in mountainous areas (up to 2000 m altitude) and in northern Europe; otherwise very rare, should be protected.
Similar species: The rare *Lactarius aspideus* is smaller; its cap is also straw- to lemon-yellow, but lacks zonation and is slimy and sticky when moist; its white milk has a bitter taste and discolours slowly to lilac.

279

280

281 *Lactarius deliciosus* ☺ Saffron Milk Cap

Cap: Flat when young, then funnel-shaped with a long inrolled margin which has a bloom when young and is later bare; light salmon-orange with circular zonation; sometimes with greenish spots particularly towards the rim; slippery when moist, very mealy when dry; mostly 7-10 cm, rarely up to 15 cm in diameter.
Gills: Light orange-yellow to ochre, green when bruised, but never with any wine-red blotches; crowded. *Spores:* Light ochre.
Stem: Orange and often with water stains; somewhat mealy; usually slightly attenuated towards the base; firm flesh.
Flesh: Cream; the mild milk is carrot-red, paling when dry, after some hours it turns greyish-green, but never wine-red.
Habitat & distribution: Only below pines, mostly on chalk-free soil; locally frequent, particularly in eastern Europe.
Similar species: Lactarius sanguifluus also grows below pines, but has mild blood-red milk from the start. There is a danger of confusing the saffron milk cap with several similar species of milk cap exuding white sap, some of which have a hot taste and are inedible.

282 *Lactarius deterrimus* ☺

Cap: Flat when young, with inrolled margin, later funnel-shaped; bright orange, often with green hues; only occasionally with circular zones; up to 10 cm in diameter.
Gills: Deep orange, with wine-red or green spots when damaged; crowded. *Spores:* Light ochre.
Stem: Orange, hardly any water stains; evenly thick, soon becoming hollow.
Flesh: Light cream-orange; with a mild, carrot-red milk sap which discolours to wine-red after about 20 minutes.
Habitat & distribution: Below spruce, particularly with young plants, in the grass; the most frequent species of milk cap in western and central Europe.
Similar species: Lactarius semisanguifluus, has almost the same characteristics and can only be distinguished by its habitat; it grows below pines on chalk. There is a danger of confusing *L. deterrimus* with similar, hot tasting, inedible species with a white milk sap.

283 *Lactarius salmonicolor* ☺☒

Cap: Flat with inrolled margin when young, then funnel-shaped; evenly orange, with weak and very close zonation, rarely with green hues, slippery and shiny for most of life; mostly 6-8 cm, rarely up to 15 cm in diameter.
Gills: Orange, with wine-red spots when damaged; dense and decurrent. *Spores:* Pale ochre.
Stem: Orange; evenly thick, strong, weakly mealy, hollow at the centre, somewhat pitted.
Flesh: Ochre, with bitter, carrot-red milk sap, when this dries on the gills it discolours to wine-red within 20 minutes.
Habitat & distribution: Frequent only below silver firs, threatened with extinction, through the decrease in their population; should be protected.
Similar species: Danger of confusing *L. salmonicolor* with similar, sometimes hot tasting, inedible milk caps which contain white sap.

281

282

283

284 *Lactarius turpis* ☠ Ugly Milk Cap

Cap: Flat when young, with inrolled, somewhat felty margin, likely to be funnel-shaped when old; blackish-olive, blotchy when old; mostly 8-10 cm in diameter.
Gills: White; close together and adnate. *Spores:* Cream-yellow.
Stem: Lighter than the cap, becoming dark and blotchy with age; evenly thick.
Flesh: White, with very hot, white milk sap.
Habitat & distribution: Only below spruce on acid soils mostly on needle litter; very frequent.
An alternative scientific name for this fungus is *Lactarius necator* (the killer) and it is therefore also called murder-fungus. However, the assumption that it is poisonous is wrong. It stems from a poisoning due to *L. necator* being confused with *Amanita phalloides*, the death cap.

285 *Lactarius fuliginosus* ☠

Cap: Flat when young, funnel-shaped when old; dark brown, minutely velvety when young, without lustre and always dry; up to 8 cm in diameter.
Gills: Yellow ochre; moderately close, adnate or somewhat decurrent.
Spores: Light ochre.
Stem: Stained lighter than the cap; without furrows at the apex.
Flesh: White; with copiously flowing white milk which tastes rather bitter and turns slowly red.
Habitat & distribution: Mostly in deciduous woodlands and in mixed forests, mainly under beeches; rather frequent.
Similar species: Lactarius picinus has a darker cap which is corrugated when old and with hot, white milk. It grows in highland coniferous forests.

286 *Lactarius lignyotus* ☺

Cap: Convex, with somewhat depressed, almost always pointed umbo at the centre and long incurved margin; dark blackish-brown, turning lighter with age; wrinkly particularly towards margin; up to 6 cm in diameter.
Gills: White when young, later pale cream, rather close together.
Spores: Light ochre.
Stem: Similar colour to the cap; rather long, evenly thick, wrinkled by the decurrent gills at the tip.
Flesh: White, slowly reddening on exposure to air; with mild white milk sap.
Habitat & distribution: In coniferous forests on acid soils, mostly at higher altitudes; frequent.

287 *Lactarius acris* ☠☒

Cap: Convex when young, later mostly flat, occasionally funnel-shaped; greyish-brown to yellowish-buff; slimy when moist, otherwise velvety smooth; up to 7 cm in diameter.
Gills: Deep ochre-yellow; close together. *Spores:* Pale ochre.
Stem: White when young, later pale ochre; without lustre.
Flesh: White; with very hot white milk that turns pink on exposure to air.
Habitat & distribution: In beech forests on chalk; rather rare, do not pick.
Similar species: Lactarius pterosporus below hornbeam has a wrinkly cap and its milk turns only slowly pink.

284

left
285
right
286

287

288 *Lactarius rufus* ☠ Rufous Milk Cap

Cap: Conical when young, later flat, can be funnel-shaped when very old, almost always with a strong, pointed umbo; dark reddish-brown and covered by a bright mealy layer, not slippery; up to 8 cm in diameter.
Gills: Flesh-pink, often blotchy when old, dense and decurrent on the stem.
Spores: White.
Stem: Of similar colour as the cap; rather long, evenly thick, becoming hollow when old.
Flesh: Reddish-brown; with watery, copious and very hot white milk.
Habitat & distribution: In large masses below spruce, pine and birch on acid soils; one of the most common milk caps.
This fungus could be confused with *Lactarius volemus* (300), which can cause rather unpleasant gastric problems when eaten.
Similar species: Lactarius quietus (292), the oak milk cap, is distinguished by a zoned cap and having bitter milk; it grows below oaks.

289 *Lactarius helvus* ☠ Maggi Fungus

Cap: Flat when young, soon funnel-shaped and occasionally with a broad, indistinct umbo; mostly reddish-ochre when young with small felty scales, becoming bare when old, often with wavily contorted rim, paling to buff; up to 15 cm in diameter.
Gills: Yellowish when young, later deep ochre-yellow to flesh-coloured; rather close together, somewhat decurrent. *Spores:* Pale yellowish.
Stem: Same colour as the cap; strong, evenly thick and minutely downy, becoming hollow when old.
Flesh: Reddish-ochre; with a watery, white mild milk sap which soon dries; odourless when young, later with a strong smell of Maggi or liquorish, particularly on drying.
Habitat & distribution: In moist, boggy conifer forests, mostly below scattered birches; not rare.
When larger quantities are consumed, this fungus can cause vomiting.

∘ 290 *Lactarius camphoratus* ☠ Curry-scented Milk Cap

Cap: Dark chestnut-brown when young and usually with a small umbo, later funnel-shaped, becoming lighter on drying; margin somewhat ridged by the gills when old, never slippery; up to 5 cm in diameter.
Gills: Light reddish-ochre, distant, dusted white by the spores when old.
Spores: Yellowish.
Stem: Same colour as the cap; thin and slender, mostly curved, somewhat attenuated at the base.
Flesh: Reddish-brown; with white, mild and watery milk, which has often dried up when the mushroom is old; smelling of Maggi or liquorish when old.
Habitat & distribution: In large groups in coniferous and mixed forests; very frequent.
Similar species: Lactarius thejogalus has a lighter orange-brown, funnel-shaped cap, which is often turned up when old; grows in moist and boggy deciduous woodland and coniferous forests, often in large numbers. The watery-white, mild or bitter milk turns slowly sulphur yellow in air.

288

289

290

291 *Lactarius torminosus* ☠ Woolly Milk Cap

Cap: Depressed, navel-like at centre with a deeply inrolled margin, later somewhat funnel-shaped; flesh-pink to brownish with circular zones, shaggy mainly at the margin; up to 12 cm in diameter.
Gills: Pale cream, close and somewhat decurrent. *Spores:* Light yellow.
Stem: Pale pink, evenly thick, becoming hollow.
Flesh: White to pale pink, with white, very hot milk.
Habitat & distribution: Only below birches, mainly on acid and moist soil; frequent.
When cooked or eaten raw, this fungus causes severe stomach and abdominal problems. In eastern Europe it is made edible by being fermented in lactic acid. In Finland it is considered edible and well liked, once treated in this way.
Similar species: Lactarius pubescens also grows under birches, but in more moist areas. Its smaller cap has no zonation, is less shaggy and more pale, often almost white. It is far more rare.

292 *Lactarius quietus* ☠ Oak Milk Cap

Cap: Flat when young, with inrolled margin, later somewhat funnel-shaped; light reddish-brown and slippery when young, buff when old, weakly circular zoning, up to 8 cm in diameter.
Gills: Dark creamy-red; dense. *Spores:* Pale yellowish.
Stem: Of same colour as the cap; evenly thick with attenuated base.
Flesh: Light reddish-brown, with watery, yellowish-white, mild milk sap, unpleasant smell of honeydew.
Habitat & distribution: Mostly in large numbers, only under oaks, very frequent.
Similar species: Lactarius rufus (288), the rufous milk cap, has a darker, red-brown, always umbonate cap without zonation, very hot milk and grows in coniferous forests.

293 *Lactarius chrysorheus* ☠

Cap: Flat, with inrolled margin when young, later indistinctly funnel-shaped; cream-yellow to light orange with circular zonation particularly towards the rim; up to 7 cm in diameter.
Gills: Light cream; dense. *Spores:* Pale ochre.
Stem: Same colour as the cap or white; rather short, evenly thick or slightly attenuated at the base.
Flesh: White, with hot white milk sap which immediately discolours bright sulfur yellow in air.
Habitat & distribution: In deciduous woodland under oak or sweet chestnut, but has also been seen under pine and on sandy soil; rather rare.
Similar species: Several orange-coloured milk caps with zonated caps look similar. Some milk caps have orange-red milk sap; the mild tasting *L. porninsis* (301) has white milk sap.
The cap of *L. insulsus* measures up to 15 cm in diameter, it has orange-pink zones, and is deeply funnel-shaped with far inrolled margin, the milk sap is extremely hot. It grows under oak or hornbeam on chalk.

291

292

293

294 *Lactarius musteus* ☠ ☒ Heath Milk Cap

Cap: Convex to funnel-shaped, with long inrolled margin which is felty when young; whitish to pale ochre, sometimes zoned and blotchy, weakly striped when old, very slippery when moist; up to 8 cm in diameter.
Gills: Dirty white when young, later pale cream, rust-brown when bruised; rather dense and decurrent when old. *Spores:* Yellowish-ochre.
Stem: Whitish-ochre and often blotchy, can be pink at the tip; hollow, strong.
Flesh: Whitish with white, mild milk which usually discolours sulphur yellow when dry.
Habitat & distribution: Only under pines mostly on sand and in fens; very rare, should be protected.

295 *Lactarius pyrogalus* ☠

Cap: Convex and slippery when young, later broad, bowl-shaped, often wavily contorted at the rim, almost dry; dirty grey, sometimes also with a violet hue; always with circular zones; up to 10 cm in diameter.
Gills: Whitish when young, later pale ochre; rather dense and decurrent.
Spores: Light ochre.
Stem: Same colour as the cap, with attenuated base.
Flesh: Watery whitish; with hot white milk sap which does not discolour on drying.
Habitat & distribution: Under broad-leaved trees, mainly under oak, hornbeam, ash and elm; not rare.

296 *Lactarius trivialis* ☠

Cap: Flat or somewhat depressed at the centre when young, with long inrolled margin, very slippery; steel blue to violet when young, marbled and with water stains at the margin, growing pale when old and then orange flesh-coloured; mostly 8-12 cm, rarely up to 25 cm in diameter.
Gills: Whitish-grey, ochre when old, with grey-green blotches when damaged; moderately dense. *Spores:* Pale yellow.
Stem: Pale ochre; slippery; mostly rather long, evenly thick.
Flesh: Whitish, with copious hot white milk sap.
Habitat & distribution: In moist coniferous forests and fens; very frequent in eastern Europe, rarer elsewhere.
The fungus can be made edible by long rinsing or fermenting and is used for culinary purposes in eastern Europe.

297 *Lactarius uvidus* ☠

Cap: Convex when young, soon flat or indistinctly funnel-shaped; dirty violet-grey when young, flesh-brown when old, occasionally with weak circular zones towards the margin, very slippery; up to 10 cm in diameter.
Gills: Whitish when young, yellowish when old; dense. *Spores:* Yellowish.
Stem: Whitish; somewhat furrowed, slippery; rather long.
Flesh: A light, fleshy brown; with copiously running, bitter milk, which discolours violet in air.
Habitat & distribution: In fens, moist deciduous woodlands and coniferous forests; at a wide range of altitudes; not rare.

294

left
295
right
296

297

298 *Lactarius mitissimus* ☠

Cap: Convex with depressed and frequently small umbo at the centre; evenly orange; with smooth, not striped, surface; up to 5 cm in diameter.
Gills: White when young, soon light cinnamon; dense. *Spores:* Pale yellow.
Stem: Orange, with an ochre-coloured mealy bloom when young.
Flesh: Yellow to orange; copious mild white milk.
Habitat & distribution: Mostly in coniferous forests; very frequent.

299 *Lactarius rubrocinctus* ☠

Cap: Soon deeply funnel-shaped with long inrolled margin, sometimes with a pointed umbo, fox-orange, turning pale when dry, occasionally furrowed at the centre, up to 8 cm in diameter.
Gills: Flesh-coloured, often with a lilac hue, dense. *Spores:* Cream-yellow.
Stem: Same colour as the cap, evenly thick, often with a darker red, ring-like zone at the apex below the gills.
Flesh: Reddish-brown; with watery, bitter to rather hot white milk.
Habitat & distribution: Mostly singly under beech; rather rare.

300 *Lactarius volemus* ☺

Cap: Flat or funnel-shaped when young; beautifully orange to brown and minutely velvety; up to 12 cm in diameter.
Gills: Pale ochre, blotchy when damaged; dense and decurrent when old.
Spores: White.
Stem: Orange-brown and with a fine bloom.
Flesh: With copiously flowing mild white milk sap and typically fishy smell.
Habitat & distribution: In deciduous and coniferous forests; frequent.
Use: Suitable only for frying.
Similar species: There is a danger of confusing *L. volemus* with numerous, similarly coloured, very hot species of lactarius; the fishy smell distinguishes *L. volemus*.

301 *Lactarius porninsis* ☺

Cap: With somewhat depressed middle and inrolled margin when young, can be funnel-shaped when old; evenly orange, mostly zonated; margin bare; up to 8 cm in diameter.
Gills: Dark cream-ochre; rather dense. *Spores:* Pale ochre.
Stem: Light orange-red; evenly thick, becoming hollow with age.
Flesh: Whitish-ochre; with mild or bitter white milk.
Habitat & distribution: Only under larch; frequent only on higher ground.

302 *Lactarius ichoratus* ☠

Cap: Flat, with inrolled margin when young, can be funnel-shaped when old; dark fox-brown in the middle, margin delineated with lighter orange-brown; somewhat shiny; up to 8 cm in diameter.
Gills: Pale ochre; rather dense. *Spores:* Pale ochre.
Stem: Orange-brown; evenly thick.
Flesh: With rather bitter, white milk.
Habitat & distribution: In deciduous woodland, predominantly below beech.

left
298
right
299

300

left
301
right
302

303 *Lactarius blennius* ☠ Slimy Milk Cap

Cap: Inrolled when young, soon funnel-shaped and often contorted at the margin, can be lobed or notched when old; evenly grey to grey-green and only rarely with indistinct circular zones; very slippery when young, later usually dry and glossy; up to 7 cm in diameter, rarely larger.
Gills: White when young, later pale cream, becoming blotchy brownish-grey when bruised; decurrent. *Spores:* Pale yellow.
Stem: Same colour as the cap, often slippery when young, with some long veins, soon becoming hollow.
Flesh: White; with copious, very hot white milk.
Habitat & distribution: In large groups in beech woods; frequent.
Similar species: Lactarius glutinopallens grows under silver fir, mostly on chalk. Its cap is more slimy and evenly light grey; it also has very hot, white milk. *L. vietus*, the grey milk cap, grows under birch. It has a more violet-grey, also slimy cap and extremely hot white milk sap which discolours grey-green when dry.

304 *Lactarious fluens* ☠

Cap: Flat when young, umbonate with inrolled margin, often funnel-shaped when old; mostly olive but also greyish-green or buff; very slippery when young, with a whitish bloom, distinct circular zonation and often with dark water stains at the margin; up to 8 cm, rarely 12 cm in diameter.
Gills: Yellowish-white, turning brownish when damaged; crowded. *Spores:* Yellowish.
Stem: Same colour with the cap, slippery only when moist, evenly thick.
Flesh: White, turning brown in the stem with age; with copious, rather hot, white milk.
Habitat & distribution: In beech woods; rather frequent.
Similar species: Lactarius pyrogalus (295), has a less slippery, more violet-grey cap. *L. uvidus* (297) can look similar, but can be distinguished by its milk which immediately discolours to violet when touched.

305 *Lactarius pallidus* ☠

Cap: Flat when young, with somewhat depressed centre, soon funnel-shaped; of evenly pale fleshy-pink, sometimes indistinctly zonated near margin only when young; very slimy when moist, glossy when dry; up to 10 cm in diameter.
Gills: Pale ochre, rarely blotchy; rather crowded. *Spores:* Pale ochre.
Stem: Paler than the cap; slippery and mostly rather short and stout, evenly thick, soon hollow.
Flesh: Pale flesh-coloured; with rather copious mild white milk sap and a weak fruity scent.
Habitat & distribution: In deciduous woodland, mainly near beech; rather frequent.
Similar species: Lactarius hysginus grows under birch among grass. Its cap is darker buff to reddish-ochre and also slimy; it is much more rare.

303

304

305

306 *Pycnoporus cinnabarinus* ☠

Cap: Semicircular, positioned sideways on wood, usually close and tile-like above one another, confluent with neighbouring caps; rather flat, a little furrowed when young; bright cinnabar-red, fruit bodies develop a brownish-red margin after winter; to 8 cm in diameter.
Pores: Cinnabar-red; quite narrow.
Flesh: Cinnabar-red, tough.
Habitat & distribution: Annual, seldom biennial: on stumps and dead branches of various deciduous trees, prefers beech and birch, mostly at higher altitudes.

307 *Laetiporus sulphureus* ☠ Sulphur Polypore

Cap: Rather flat, top wavy and bare; bright sulphur-yellow when young, with light margin, later paling to a dirty whitish-grey; up to 30 cm in diameter.
Pores: Light sulphur-yellow, often with yellow drops when young, very narrow, 2-4 mm long.
Flesh: Yellow, soft and juicy when young, turning pale after death of fungus; crumbly, with unpleasant smell and bitter taste.
Habitat & distribution: On living trees, mainly oak, willow and various fruit trees; annual, growing for several subsequent years on one trunk. The mycelium of this dangerous parasite transforms heartwood into brown mess. The trunk is hollowed out from below and once fruit bodies show, the tree is lost. The caps extend like tiles above one another and can form series of up to 400 caps. Dead fruit bodies persist on the trunk.

308 *Phaeolus spadiceus* ☠

Cap: Originating from a misshapen lump, fan shapes then spread and grow tile-like above one another; soft with light yellow border, covered when young with a white, later red-brown and eventually with a black felt.
Pores: Yellow-green when young, blotchy when bruised, dark brown when old and splitting like gills.
Flesh: Yellowish-brown when young, soft, juicy, later rusty-brown. Drying after death of fungus; very light.
Habitat & distribution: On a variety of coniferous trees, mainly pine and larch; mostly at base of living trunks.
This fungus penetrates the heart wood of a tree via the roots and initiates a heavy attack of brown, cubical rot. The annual fruit bodies appear for some years after the death of the tree.

306

307

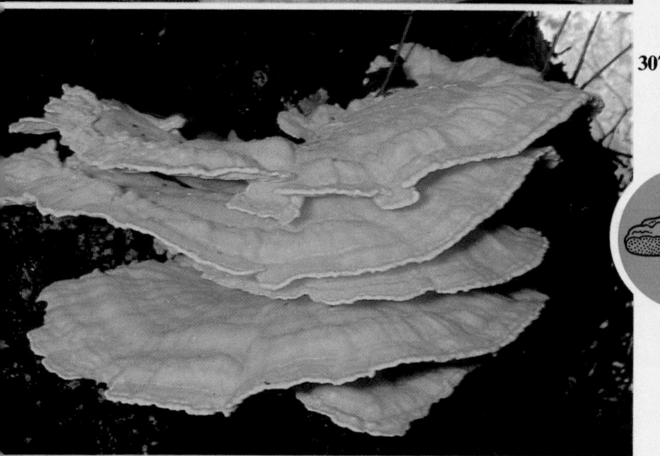

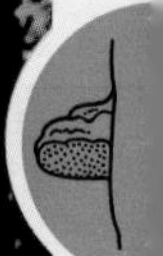

308

309 *Trametes versicolor* ☠

Cap: Flat, semicircular with bulky point of attachment, caps usually grow tile-like above one another; colour changeable, from whitish-grey to yellow and often black when mature in late autumn, it also has brown or greenish zones, and looks rather colourful; covered by silky, glossy zones made up of very short hairs; up to 8 cm in diameter.
Pores: White, rather wide.
Flesh: White; leathery and tough from the start.
Habitat & distribution: Throughout the year in deciduous forests, mainly on beech stumps, favours sunny areas; very frequent.
Similar species: T. zonata is much more rare; its point of attachment is even larger; silky hair absent. *T.hirsuta* (318) is more massive, its cap is rough-haired, it grows in sunny positions on dead deciduous trees. *Auricularia mesenterica* (373) is similar, but is distinguished by its greyish-brown underside.
The genus *Tramete* includes about 12 species with flat, semicircular fruit bodies which grow on dead wood. In contrast to other polypores, which often form large fruit bodies that exist for several years, the trametes are annual, so fruit bodies soon die and become very light and tough. Most fungi with a pore-like fruit layer are commonly called polypores. As pores are not a characteristic which indicate a true relationship between species, the polypores are classified in different families. Those with cap and stem are not closely related to those extending from wood like shelves.

310 *Spongiporus subcaesius* ☠

Cap: Semicircular, with narrow, compact place of attachment; caps above one another, singly or in groups; dark bluish-grey when young, with white margin; turning pale dirty-grey when old, mostly with furrows from point of origin to margin; up to 8 cm in diameter.
Pores: White; narrow.
Flesh: White; very soft and juicy when young, can exude bitter water; tough and very light when dry.
Habitat & distribution: Annual on debarked, deciduous wood; frequent.
Similar species: Spongiporus caesius is somewhat darker blue; and distinguished by growing exclusively on coniferous wood. Predominantly found on the cutting plane of sawn timber that is hollowed by root rot. A number of other polypores with initially pure white, soft and watery flesh grow on various deciduous and coniferous woods. *Spongiporus stypticus* is recognized most easily. It is found frequently on dead pine stumps, has larger caps and its flesh tastes very bitter.

309

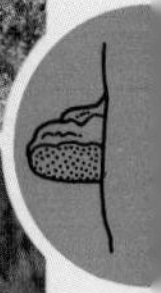

310

311 *Heterobasidion annosum* ☠ Root Fomes

Cap: Very narrow, often extending only 1-2 cm from wood, growing tile-like above one another; dark brown, zoned, white margin when young, bare, with grooves like separate swellings, very hard, up to 15 cm across.
Pores: White when young, later yellowish; narrow.
Flesh: White; hard and tough, with acrid smell.
Habitat & distribution: Very frequent on coniferous wood; causes bad brown rot in the heart wood of living trees. Fruit bodies appear after tree is dead.

312 *Trichaptum abietinum* ☠

Cap: Semicircular, growing tile-like above one another; whitish-grey, felty and somewhat zoned; very thin flesh; up to 3 cm across.
Pores: Near stem exending long tubes; violet near margin.
Habitat & distribution: Annual, late autumn on conifers, frequent.

313 *Meripilus giganteus* Giant Polypore

Cap: Fan-shaped, with stem; often forming large fruit bodies with neighbouring caps, tile-like above one another; dark brown with yellowish-brown, zoned edge; up to 20 cm across.
Pores: Pale yellowish; narrow.
Flesh: White at first, soft and succulent, turning blackish later.
Habitat & distribution: Annual, mainly on stumps of beech and oak.

314 *Inonotus radiatus* ☠

Cap: Grow shelf-like above one another; at first yellowish-brown, minutely felty, often exuding brown drops, later bare, dark yellowish brown, almost black when old; up to 6 cm across.
Pores: Brown, with silvery shine at the edge; rather narrow.
Flesh: Dark red-brown; hard, tough.
Habitat & distribution: Annual on living alder trunks, can kill trees fast.

315 *Fomitopsis pinicola* ☠

Cap: Thick, shelf-like; with crust, at first shiny yellowish-brown, later matt red-brown, black when old, often with zones in three colours; fruit bodies last several years; up to 20 cm across.
Pores: Straw-coloured; very narrow.
Flesh: Pale yellowish-brown, acrid smell when young.
Habitat & distribution: On pine and alder, at higher altitudes.

316 *Piptoporus betulinus* Birch Polypore

Cap: Spherical when young, later cushion-like, with a stem-like attachment to wood; first white, then hazel-brown; up to 15 cm across.
Pores: Whitish-grey, not blotchy; narrow.
Flesh: First white, soft, succulent; tough when old and very light.
Habitat & distribution: On standing and toppled birch trunks.
This fungus attacks weakened trees and initiates intensive brown rot; fruit bodies appear after the death of the tree.

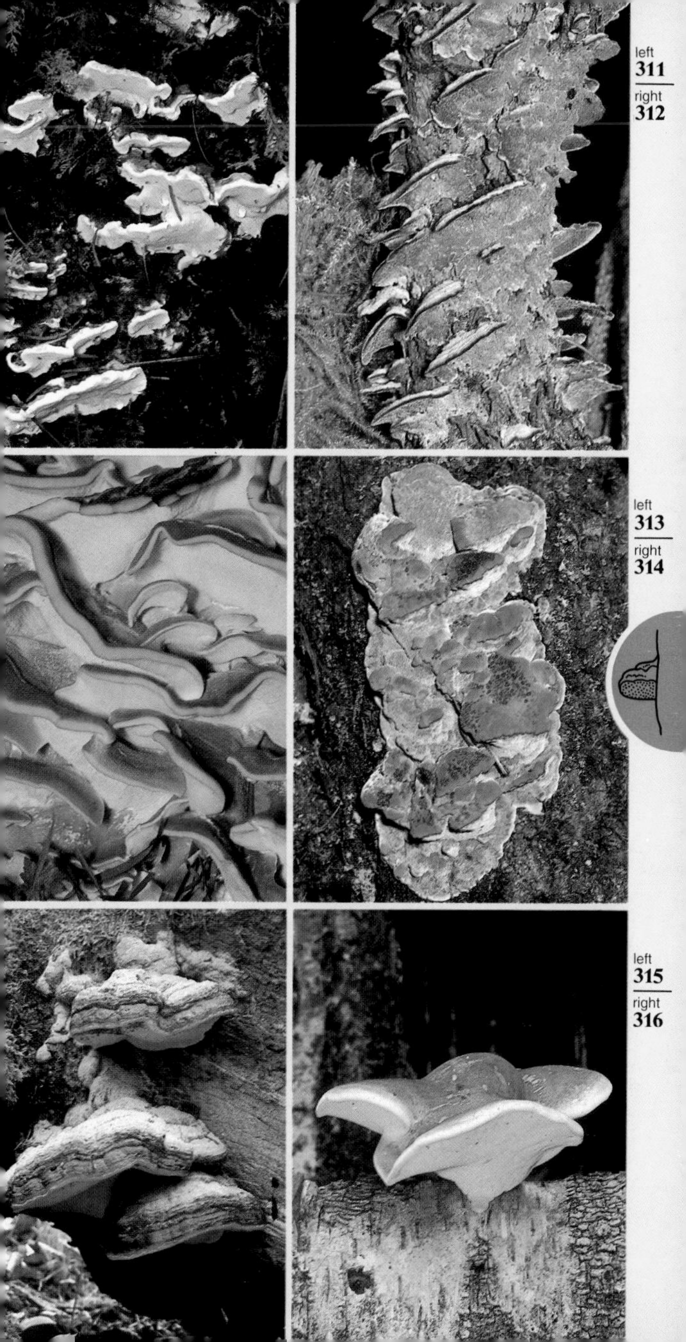

left
311
right
312

left
313
right
314

left
315
right
316

317 *Daedaleopsis confragosa*

Blood-stained Bracket

Cap: Semicircular, on wood, rather flat, pale brownish, minutely velvety, mostly furrowed, with several zones, sometimes reddening under pressure, especially on margin; up to 10 cm across.
Pores: Dirty-white, reddening under pressure; very variable: thick-walled, wide, but can also be also gill-like: there are many transitional forms.
Flesh: Light brown, very tough.
Habitat & distribution: Mostly on dead trunks of willow and alder, more rare on other deciduous woods; frequent.
Because the fruit layer resembles pores or gills, this fungus has been repeatedly split into different species.

318 *Trametes hirsuta* ☠

Cap: Plate-like, round; oval when growing unilaterally; blunt edge; surface whitish-grey to brownish and densely velvety; distinctly zoned; up to 8 cm across.
Pores: Whitish-grey, can be darker grey or yellowish when old; rather wide and thick-walled.
Flesh: White; tough, rather light.
Habitat & distribution: Often in extended lawns, exclusively on wood of dead deciduous trees; in sunny spots; frequent everywhere.
Similar species: Trametes gibbosa forms larger fruit bodies.
and has an only minutely felty surface. It is distinguished by the thick, tuber-like point of attachment; it grows on beech stumps.

319 *Gloeophyllum odoratum* ☠

Cap: At first misshapen and bulbous, later shelf-like, furrowed and minutely woolly, often confluent with neighbouring caps; bright yellow-brown at margin, older parts black-brown; to 10 cm across.
Pores: Yellowish-white; very large and wide.
Flesh: Yellowish-brown; very hard, tough; gives off pleasantly sweet smell reminiscent of aniseed or fennel when broken.
Habitat & distribution: Exclusively on stumps of old pines, rarely silver firs; rare at low altitudes, otherwise frequent.

320 *Fomes fomentarius* ☠ **Tinder Fungus**

Cap: Tuberous when young, soon broadly hoof-shaped, very hard and thick; with light grey, somewhat zoned surface, pale brown at margin; up to 35 cm across.
Pores: Whitish-grey, very narrow, blotchy when bruised on the fresh fruit body, red brown when cut; in older fungi very thick and in several layers upon one another.
Flesh: Yellowish-brown; soft and tough, rather thin between the crust of the cap and the layer of pores; burning easily (has been used in the past for the production of tinder).
Habitat & distribution: Mostly on dying beech, rarely on birch or other deciduous trees; frequent.

317

left
318
right
319

320

321 *Stereum hirsutum* ☠ Yellow Stereum

Cap: Rather thin and wavily contorted, often confluent with neighbouring caps and trailing down wood; at first bright orange-yellow, covered with thick felty hair, pales to greyish-white later; 1-2 mm thick, extending 1-2 cm from wood.
Fruit layer: Light orange-yellow, not reddening under pressure, smooth, no pores.
Habitat & distribution: On dead wood of deciduous (rarely coniferous) trees, frequent everywhere.
Similar species: Stereum rugosum forms extended fruit bodies, with only narrow cap edges; its fruit layer reddens on rubbing. *Stereum sanguinolentum* is very thin and grey; it grows on coniferous wood and its fruit layer turns dark red when rubbed.

322 *Hymenochaete rubiginosa* ☠

Cap: Very thin, connected to wood only at the centre and thus somewhat bell-shaped, caps extend to 2 cm shelves from wood in a dense tile arrangement; dark red-brown with narrow black zones.
Fruit layer: Dark red-brown; smooth, its pointed bristles can only be seen at large magnification; mostly extending down tree and fused with lower caps; some forms only encrust, without zonating cap edges.
Flesh: Dark brown; tough.
Habitat & distribution: Mostly on stumps or upright dead trees (oak or sweet chestnut); not rare.
Similar species: Hymenochaete tabacina grows predominantly on willow and hazel. It often forms rows of confluent caps, their surface is dark brown and yellow close to the edge.

323 *Phellinus punctatus* ☠

Fruit body: On the underside of thick branches and trunks of dying willows; forms a crust when young, becomes bolster-shaped over the years with as new fruit layers grow, often covers large areas; dark red-brown.
Pores: Shimmering silkily in slanting sunlight; very narrow.
Flesh: Dark red-brown; very tough and firm.
Similar species: The different species of *Phellinus* may form shelf-like fruit bodies or just coat the wood underside.

324 *Hymenochaete cruenta* ☠ ☒

Fruit body: Flat, very thin (to only 0.4 mm thick), margins free, becoming oval or circular; up to 3 cm across.
Fruit layer: Bright blood-red, brown-red when dead; smooth with small bumps, pointed bristles visible with a strong lens.
Habitat & distribution: On newly dead branches of firs whilst still on the tree, often high above the ground; rare and should be protected.

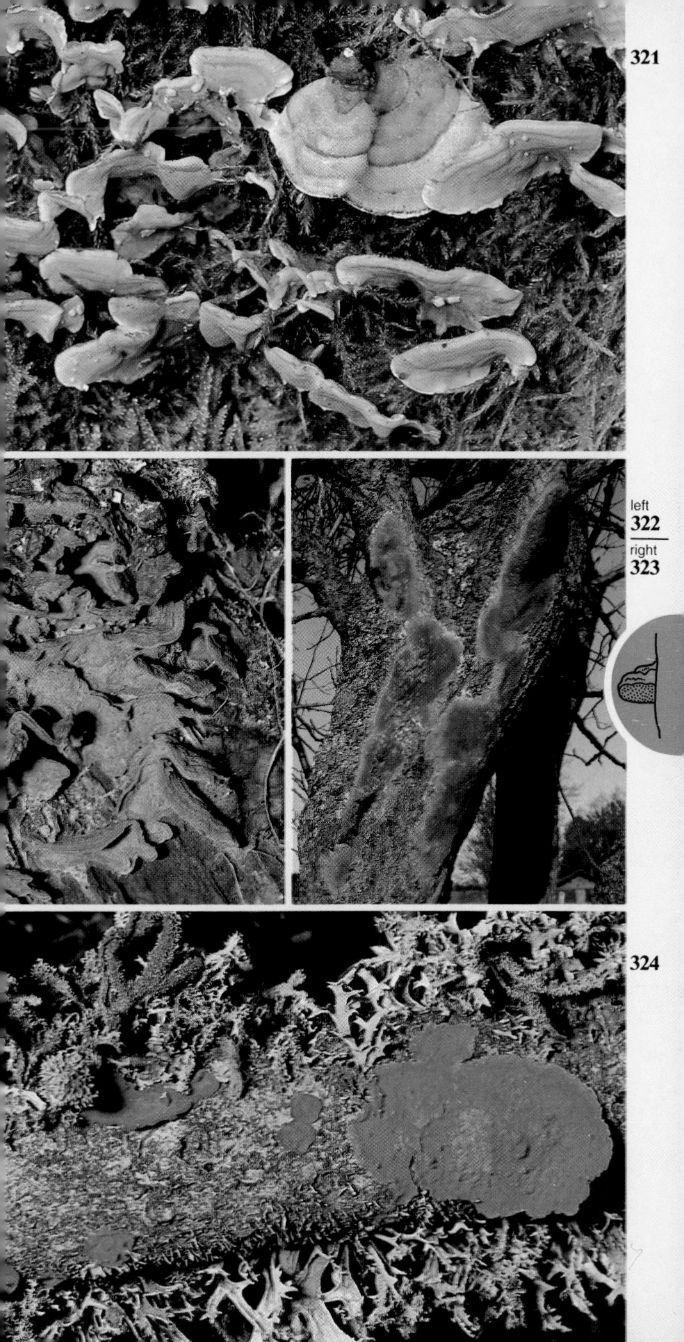

321

left
322
right
323

324

325 *Gloeophyllum sepiarium* ☠

Cap: Semicircular, very rough with weakly circular zonation; dark brown, red-brown towards the margin, with yellowish-brown extending edge when young, up to 6 cm across.
Pores: Yellow when young, rust-brown when old; very wide and thick-walled, usually stretched apart like gills.
Flesh: Red-brown; very hard and tough.
Habitat & distribution: On debarked coniferous wood (fir, pine), mainly on fence posts, banisters and wooden benches; very frequent.
The fungus causes brown rot in the heart wood; it is one of the most dangerous destructive agents of exposed coniferous building wood; can cope with desiccation. Often found in sunny, warm locations.

326 *Merulius tremellosus* ☠ Jelly Rot

Cap: Forms long tile-like rows above one another, shell-shaped when single; whitish-grey, roughly felty, transparently orange when moist; very broad.
Fruit layer: Orange-yellow when young, turning pale when old; with folds, forked, often with honey-comb markings.
Flesh: Orange-yellow; flexible and jelly-like, dry: tough like cartilage.
Habitat & distribution: In late autumn and winter on stumps of various deciduous trees, mainly on beech; not rare.
The dreaded wet rot *Serpula lacrymans* is also a bracket fungus. Its fungal hyphae can penetrate structural wood and cause a great deal of damage in buildings. Its fruit bodies, up to one square metre in extent, are spread flat on the wood; their yellowish-brown, wavy folds are surrounded by a white, cotton wool-like weave of mycelial threads.

327 *Plicatura crispa* ☠

Cap: At first bell-shaped, then hanging irregularly shell- or bowl-shaped, minutely felty when young; zoned yellow- or reddish- brown, with white rim; tough and very thin; up to 2 cm across.
Fruit layer: White; irregularly veined and folded, mostly forked.
Habitat & distribution: In large numbers on beech wood, mainly on thin, dead yet standing trees; usually in autumn and winter; frequent.

328 *Phlebia merismoides* ☠

Fruit body: Flat, spread and fused with the wood; irregularly circular with fibrous growth margin, often confluent and covering large areas; has narrow margins when grows on vertical wood.
Fruit layer: Bright orange-red when young, later pale, dirty flesh-brown; folded and wrinkly, often with bumps.
Flesh: Tough, jelly-like; without scent or taste.
Habitat & distribution: From late autumn to spring on the underside of still firm wood of deciduous trees; mostly on fallen trees or on stumps of beech and birch; causes severe white rot; frequent.

325

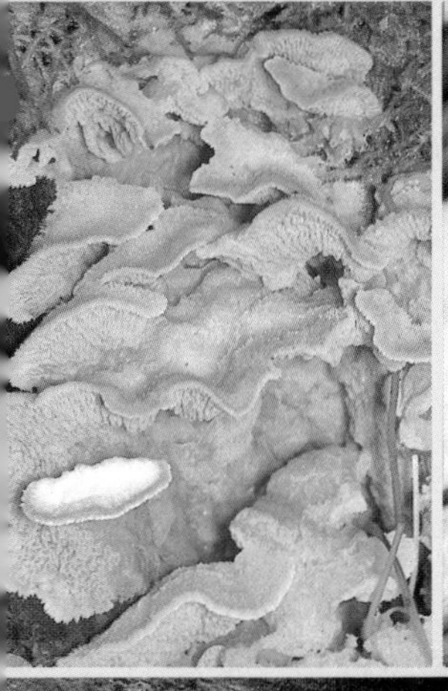

left **326**

right **327**

328

329 *Ramaria largentii* ☺☒

Fruit body: Forked repeatedly, with strong, short, cream-coloured stem and vertical branches that are blunt or forked at the tip which are evenly lemon- to golden-yellow, pale yellow-ochre when old; 6-10 cm broad and up to 12 cm high.
Flesh: White; without scent, mild taste.
Habitat & distribution: Predominantly in coniferous forests at higher altitudes, but also in deciduous woodlands and mixed forests; rather frequent in mountainous areas, otherwise rare. *Ramaria largentii* is edible but tough and not particularly useful for cooking.
Similar species: It is almost impossible to distinguish the mature fruit bodies of *Ramaria formosa* (332) externally. Therefore, in the interests of safety, no coral fungi should be eaten.

330 *Ramaria flaccida* ☠

Fruit body: Forked repeatedly, rather slim, with many steeply vertical, slim branches and thin, very short, rather pointed twigs; evenly ochre; up to 4 cm broad and just as high.
Flesh: White; somewhat bitter taste.
Habitat & distribution: In large numbers in coniferous forests, mainly below pine and fir, mostly in new plantations on shed needles; very frequent.

331 *Calocera viscosa* ☠ Jelly Antler Fungus

Fruit body: Mostly simply branched, not split or antler-like branches, white and felty at the base, rooting very deeply in the wood, rather slender; bright egg-yellow to orange, surface often white, mealy and somewhat sticky; up to 3 cm broad and 6 cm high.
Flesh: Yellowish-white; elastic, tough and bendable; without scent or taste.
Habitat & distribution: On dead coniferous wood, very frequent.
C. viscosa is deemed, wrongly, to belong to the coral fungi. Although its tough flesh is tasteless and indigestible, it rarely seems to lead to gastric complaints.

332 *Ramaria formosa* ☠ Yellow Tipped Coral

Fruit body: Branched like coral, 8-12 cm broad, stem 2-3 cm thick; first white, later flesh-coloured; branches upright, egg-yellow when young, later turning pale, with many short and blunt yellow branch tips which pale only when old.
Flesh: White, reddening with age, no scent, slightly bitter taste.
Habitat & distribution: Mostly in large groups or circles in deciduous woodlands and in mixed forests; rather frequent.
Consumption of the poisonous *R. formosa* often causes gastric problems.
Similar species: Ramaria flava is distinguished by uniformly ochre-yellow colours; it also grows in deciduous woodlands.

329

left
330

right
331

332

333 *Ramaria botrytis* ☺☒ Clustered Coral

Fruit body: Consists of a thick, almost tuberous white or pale-yellowish stem which attenuates downward; it has several thick and densely crowded branches which bend outward; with short twigs of reddish hue at the tip; up to 12 cm broad and just as high.
Flesh: White, rather soft, succulent when young; no scent, bitter taste.
Habitat & distribution: Singly or in groups, in deciduous and mixed forests, mainly under beeches; rare and should be protected.
Similar species: Pale fruit bodies can lose the red colour at their branch tips and can then easily be confused with *R. pallida* (334).

334 *Ramaria pallida* ☠

Fruit body: Branched like coral, with short and weak stem; cream-yellow when young, soon dirty grey-ochre, with long, upright, somewhat furrowed branches and short twigs which are pale lilac at their tips; up to 15 cm high and equally wide.
Flesh: White, with weak soapy smell and slightly bitter taste.
Habitat & distribution: Predominantly in deciduous woodland under beech, more rarely in coniferous forests, mainly in mountainous areas; rather rare.
This fungus is not dangerously poisonous, but has a strong laxative effect even when eaten in small amounts, and is therefore inedible.
Similar species: Besides pale forms of *R. botrytis*, fruit bodies of the poisonous *R.formosa* can look deceptively similar to *R.pallida*. *R. flava* is also similar, it grows in beech forests; is yellow-ochre and its twigs never have lilac tips.

335 *Clavulina cinerea* ☠ Grey Coral Fungus

Fruit body: Slim, short, tuberous stem and thick branches which divide only near their tips where they are usually bent; dirty grey-violet, more ash-grey when old; 3-10 cm high and also broad.
Flesh: Dirty greyish-white; brittle, without scent or taste.
Habitat & distribution: In deciduous and coniferous forests, mainly at higher altitudes; rather frequent.
Similar species: Clavaria rugosa is smaller, pale greyish-white and grows in large groups in fir forests. The slender, longitudinally furrowed fruit bodies are often twisted lengthways and parted at their tips in short, blunt twigs, more rarely they are also found undivided.

333

334

335

336 *Pterula multifida* ☠ ☒

Fruit body: Parted from the base and extending into many narrow, pointed twigs, stem absent; mostly upright at an angle or growing along the ground; at first whitish-grey, then dirty greyish-ochre; forming lawns up to 20 cm wide.
Flesh: Smells strongly and unpleasantly of garlic.
Habitat & distribution: Usually forming mostly large lawns with a spiky surface, in coniferous forests among moss and needle litter, generally rare and should be protected.

337 *Clavulina coralloides* ☠

Fruit body: With rather small, whitish and minutely pruinose stem and branches that end in short twiglets; the branches are white at first, later pale brownish and finally flattened and occasionally long and drawn out; up to 4 cm high.
Flesh: White; somewhat fibrous, mild taste.
Habitat & distribution: Usually in large numbers, often forming lawns; in deciduous and coniferous forest; frequent.

338 *Thelephora terrestris* ☠ Earth Fan

Cap: Funnel-shaped, often several caps grow like tiles above one another, they narrow into the stem; rough and felty, the margin is white at first, later irregularly lobed, contorted, dark rusty-brown and not zoned, grey-brown to black when old; to 4 cm broad.
Fruit layer: Dark grey-brown, rough with bumpy warts and ray-like grooves, minutely pruinose when young.
Stem: Dark brownish-black; short.
Flesh: Grey-brown, blackening when old; soon very tough, bendable.
Habitat & distribution: Usually in large numbers on moist and mossy forest floors, occasionally growing up on fallen twigs and branches; very frequent.
Similar species: *Thelephorea anthocephala* has a cap which is split up into frayed lobes that are rusty-brown with a whitish margin and grows occasionally in moist deciduous woodlands. The earth fan family contains only a few species and is closely related to the coral fungi group. All species have a tough, leathery flesh which can sometimes smell rather unpleasant.

339 *Thelephora palmata* ☠

Fruit body: Multiple coral-like branching with twigs that are flat and incised at the end; almost white when very young, soon dark black-brown, overcast with dirty lilac-brown, although the branch ends remain whitish; up to 6 cm broad and just as high.
Flesh: Black-brown; very tough and firm, smelling unpleasantly of garlic.
Habitat & distribution: Mostly in groups, in coniferous forests among moss and needle litter; rather frequent.

336

left
337

right
338

339

340 *Sparassis crispa* ☺ Cauliflower Fungus

Fruit body: Rounded, resembling a cauliflower in shape; a rough stem originates from a hard underground nodule; its many branches end in thick, drawn out and wavy lobes; almost white when young, pale yellow or reddish-brown later; up to over 30 cm broad and weighing up to 5 kg.
Flesh: White; rather soft and brittle, with pleasant, spicy scent and mild taste.
Habitat & distribution: In pine forests on the thick main roots at the base of old pines; where the fruit body has not been cut off too low, it can regenerate for many years; not rare.

341 *Sparassis brevipes* ☺☒

Fruit body: In colour and size like *S. crispa*, but the ends of its branches are thinner, more broadly drawn out and wavy; white when young, becoming cream later.
Flesh: White; mild taste and no scent.
Habitat & distribution: At the base of old silver firs; attached to their roots by a nodule; very rare and should be protected.
Similar species: A particular form growing below old oaks was formerly regarded as a separate species; it cannot, however, be distinguished from *S. brevipes*.

342 *Hericium flagellum* ☠☒

Fruit body: Branching like coral, with horizontally extending branches which are split into short twigs, with bundles of long, pointed, downward pointing spines at their tips; pure white for a long time, only at extreme age becoming cream or brownish; staying fresh for several weeks; up to 30 cm broad, and weighing several kilogrammes.
Habitat & distribution: On thick, dead silver fir trunks, almost only in mountainous areas; rather rare and should be protected.

343 *Hericium coralloides* ☠☒

Fruit body: Branching like coral, ends of twigs thin, extending horizontally and with downward-pointing spines which are arranged comb-like in a single row; white when young, later cream; up to 30 cm wide.
Habitat & distribution: On dead copper beech trunks, which are strongly decayed and debarked, the trunks may be upright or fallen over, mainly in moist places; rather rare and should be protected.
Similar species: Hericium erinaceum (hedgehog fungus) which grows on living beeches and oaks. This pure white fungus can be recognized by the thick branches which are fused in a bulbous cap and by the dense, long, white spines. Regarded as rare.

340

left
341
right
342

343

344 *Clavariadelphus pistillaris* ☠ Giant Club

Fruit body: Coarsely club-shaped; occasionally also slender or branching; rather firm and ochre-yellow when young, later a dirty ochre with a lilac-grey hue; wrinkly, soft and spongy; up to 15 cm high and 5 cm thick.
Flesh: White; rather bitter taste.
Habitat & distribution: Often in large groups in deciduous woodland, mostly below beeches; locally frequent.
Similar species: The fruit body of *C. truncatus* has a blunt end and its flesh has a mild taste, it grows predominantly in coniferous forests, particularly near silver fir. In colour and in appearance *G. truncatus* can be almost similar to *Gomphus clavatus* (347).

345 *Clavariadelphus ligula* ☠

Fruit body: Club-shaped and frequently flat, often wrinkly and hollow when old; light reddish-yellow when young, later dirty ochre, usually white and fibrous at the base; up to 5 cm high.
Flesh: White, rarely reddening; without scent, mild taste.
Habitat & distribution: Sometimes in huge numbers and occasionally connected at the base, mainly in conifer forests at higher altitudes; rather rare.

346 *Macrotyphula filiformis* ☠

Fruit body: Very thin and slender; usually unbranched, occasionally with abortive branches at the base; smooth, hollow; ochre-yellow to pale fleshy-brown, fibrous and felty at the base; up to 5 cm high, but only 1-2 mm thick.
Flesh: White; mild taste, without scent.
Habitat & distribution: Late autumn, in large groups on old beech and oak leaves, easily overlooked; not rare.
Similar species: Macrotyphula fistulosa also grows on fallen leaves in late autumn, but attains a height of 20 cm and is about 4 mm wide. It is mostly solitary and rather rare.

347 *Gomphus clavatus* ☺☒

Cap: Funnel-shaped or with an upturned margin; pale lilac when young, soon dirty lilac-grey to olive-ochre; with striped, irregularly forked ridges of a fleshy-lilac hue on the outside; up to 6 cm wide.
Stem: Ochre- to lilac-grey; attenuating towards the ground, gradually merging with the cap.
Flesh: White; soft, without scent, mild taste.
Habitat & distribution: Mostly fused into tufts and forming fairy rings, in coniferous highland forests; very rare in low lying areas, should be protected. Due to its great similarity with the club fungi, particularly the giant club, *G. clavatus* is no longer classified with the chanterelles, but forms a separate family which is regarded as most closely related to the coral fungi.

344

left
345

right
346

347

348 *Cantharellus cibarius* ☺ Chanterelle / Girolle

Cap: Convex when young, soon funnel-shaped with an irregularly contorted margin; deep egg-yellow; up to 6 cm in diameter. It has ridges which are irregularly forked, often inter-connected by cross veins, decurrent to lower stem.
Stem: Same colour as the cap; mostly attenuated and merging into the cap.
Flesh: White; with rather hot taste and pleasant smell.
Habitat & distribution: Predominantly on acid soils, in coniferous forests at higher altitudes; more rare on lower ground and probably decreasing through over collecting.
Use: Suitable for all freshly cooked meals, but difficult to digest; not for drying.
Similar species: A somewhat larger and paler variety can be found in deciduous woodlands. In mountainous areas a further form occurs which has amethyst-coloured scales on its cap.

349 *Hygrophoropsis aurantiaca* ☠

Cap: Flat when young, circular with inrolled cap minutely velvety and bright orange-yellow, later funnel-shaped and turning pale; up to 6 cm in diameter.
Gills: Bright orange, ridge-like, narrow and thick, with blunt edge, branching.
Stem: Same colour as the cap, evenly thick or attenuated, minutely velvety.
Flesh: Orange; mild taste, without scent.
Habitat & distribution: Coniferous forests and fens; frequent.
This fungus is not poisonous, but it has occasionally caused gastric problems .

350 *Craterellus cornucopioides* ☺ Horn of Plenty or Black Trumpet

Cap: Trumpet-shaped, inrolled when young, then deeply funnel-shaped, opening uninterrupted to base of stem; dark greyish-brown to almost black and somewhat scaly.
Fruit layer: First grey and smooth externally, then veined and wrinkly; up to 4 cm in diameter.
Stem: Blackish-grey; hollow.
Flesh: Black, rather tough, with earthy smell.
Habitat & distribution: Dense clusters in beech forests; frequent.
Use: Young fruit bodies edible; and a good seasoning if dried and powderized.

351 *Cantharellus tubaeformis* ☺

Cap: Trumpet-shaped, deeply umbilicate with long inrolled margin; dark grey-brown to black-brown, moderately scaly; to 5 cm in diameter. It has ridges which are beautifully yellow when young, later dirty yellowish- or whitish-grey; narrow and thick, far apart, branching, decurrent.
Stem: At first lovely yellow, then a dirty greyish-yellow and attenuating towards the base.
Flesh: Yellowish-grey; mild taste, no scent.
Habitat & distribution: Large groups in coniferous forests in moist areas; very frequent.
Similar species: Cantharellus xanthopus which has a bright orange cap underside, it grows in moist highland forests.

348
left
349
right
350
351

352 *Sarcodon imbricatus* ☺

Cap: First slightly and later fully convex, with somewhat depressed middle, margin often lobed; greyish-brown to grey-reddish and covered in large, rough scales, reminiscent of a hawk's plumage; thick flesh, to 15 cm in diameter.
Spines: White; tapering, 6-12 mm long, shorter towards margin; breaking off easily, arranged along the side of the stem.
Stem: Dirty whitish-grey; very hard and firm, notably short.
Flesh: Dirty grey; firm; with spicy scent and rather hot to bitter taste.
Habitat & distribution: Mostly in rows in coniferous forests, more rarely in deciduous woodland; frequent.
Use: Freshly prepared, the fungus tastes very hot, but dried and powderized it makes an excellent seasoning.
Similar species: There are several closely related tooth fungi which are all fairly rare. Their caps, however, have only few scales or none at all, so confusion is avoided. These species are rather tough, partly very bitter and, without exception, inedible.

353 *Hydnum repandum* ☺

Wood Hedgehog or Urchin of the Woods

Cap: Convex with thick flesh, usually irregularly contorted, with an inrolled margin when young; pale buff to orange-brown; up to 15 cm in diameter but usually much smaller.
Spines: White, later pale cream, attenuate, often proceeding down the stem.
Stem: Cream-white; mostly to one side of the cap, rather strong, sometimes with a swollen base.
Flesh: White or pale yellow, without scent, taste first mild, later bitter.
Habitat & distribution: Deciduous and coniferous forest; frequent.
Similar species: The cap of *Hydnum rufescens* is darker, more red-brown, it has an even shape and more slender stem. It grows mainly in coniferous highland forests and is often regarded only as a variety of *H. repandum.*

354 *Hydnellum peckii* ☠☒

Cap: At first slightly club-shaped, later funnel-shaped, with weakly circular zonation; white when young, minutely felty and with blood-red drops of water, later discolouring to rust- to grey-brown, margin stays pale for the longest; very hard; to 6 cm in diameter.
Spines: First white, later dirty brownish and hard.
Stem: Short, very tough and firm, minutely felty when young, of irregular shape.
Flesh: Soft and spongy at first, a blood-red, watery sap exudes when pressure is applied, later dirty flesh-brown; woody and very tough.
Habitat & distribution: Mostly in groups in coniferous forests, mainly in mountainous regions; rather rare, should be protected.
Similar species: There are several similar tooth fungi which are blue, black or brown; they also become tough with age, but don't have red sap. *Onnia tomentosa* (44) looks similar to *H. peckii*, but its fruit layer is made of pores.

352

353

354

355 *Lycoperdon perlatum* ☺ Common Puffball

Fruit body: Inverted flask-shaped with spherical top part and extended stem with folds; white when young, covered in coarse warts which can be brushed off, later discolouring to greyish-brown; up to 5 cm high and 3 cm in diameter. Ripe fruit bodies open at the apex, release their olive-brown spores and lose their surface warts.
Gleba: The interior of the young fungus is pure white and soft like cotton wool; it turns yellowish then olive, later disintegrating to spore dust; it has a radish smell when young, mild taste.
Habitat & distribution: In deciduous and coniferous forests; frequent everywhere.
All puffballs with pure white gleba are edible when young. The puffballs, commonly called 'bovists', belong to the family Gasteromycetes. Their spores do not ripen on an external surface as in other fungi, but rather within the gleba. Only when the spores are fully developed can they escape, because the apical pore opens once they are. The Gasteromycetes cover the puffballs, bovists, earth stars and birds nest fungi as well as stinkhorns and cage fungi (see p. 210).
Similar species: When young, *Lycoperdon perlatum* can be confused with both the poisonous species of *Amanita*: *A. muscaria* (150) the fly agaric, and *A. pantherina* (151) the panther. When sectioned, these can be distinguished from the common puffball by a yellow or red line at their cap.

356 *Lycoperdon pyriforme* ☺ Stump Puffball

Fruit body: Pear-shaped with spherical top gradually merging with stem; often without distinct stem; pale grey or greyish-brown when young, never pure white, covered with minute warts, bare and dark brown when old; to 4 cm high and as wide.
Gleba: Distinctly delimited from sterile stem flesh which remains white, it is first pure white, then yellowish olive; like cotton when old, spores dispersing from operculum (opening at top of fruit body).
Habitat & distribution: In clusters on stumps, pieces of wood or cones; very frequent everywhere.
Similar species: Lycoperdon spadiceum grows on meadows. It has a more distinct stalk, is lead-grey at first and then turns brown. There are several other similar species which are difficult to distinguish.

357 *Lycoperdon umbrinum* ☒

Fruit body: Spherical or egg-shaped; soot-grey and densely covered in small umber-brown warts which can be brushed off; to 3 cm wide and 4 cm high.
Gleba: First white, distinctly delimited from sterile flesh of stem, soft like cotton wool, later discolouring to olive- or purple-brown, disintegrating to spore dust which exits from operculum (opening at top of fruit body).
Habitat & distribution: Often in large groups in coniferous forests; easily overlooked; not rare.
Similar species: Lycoperdon molle is lighter grey- to coffee-brown and somewhat larger.

355
356
357

358 *Clavatia utriformis* ☺

Fruit body: Inverted pear-shaped to inverted cone-shaped with a strong stem part which attenuates towards the root; at first pure white with coarse warts, later grey, becoming blotchy; when the warts fall off, a surface pattern of polygonal fields is revealed, the top part decays with age; to 15 cm high and 10 cm wide.
Gleba: White when young, later olive-brown; brown-black when ripe, disintegrating; delimited from sterile flesh of stem.
Habitat & distribution: On fertilized meadows, only at the fringe of woods; fairly rare.
Similar species: Langermannia gigantea, giant puffball, grows in similar localities; the spherical fruit bodies attain widths of up to 50 cm; it is tasty if sliced and fried when fresh.

359 *Lycoperdon mammiforme* ☠

Fruit body: Spherical to pear-shaped; at first pure white with slightly grainy inner skin and an outer skin which disintegrates in flakes that are soon shed, later ochre, chocolate-brown when old; up to 6 cm in diameter.
Gleba: White when young and soft like cotton wool; at maturity disintegrating to an umber-brown mass of spores dispersing from the operculum (hole at the top of the fruit body).
Habitat & distribution: In beech woodlands on chalk; regarded as rare and should therefore not be collected.

360 *Clavatia excipuliformis* ☺

Fruit body: Club- to inverted flask-shaped, usually somewhat enlarged at base and with an almost spherical top, at maturity this disintegrates entirely; the released spores are olive to umber-brown. Longitudinal sections reveal a gleba which is white at first, then turns greyish-brown; the stem flesh of an old fungus is light yellowish-brown; its surface is covered evenly with pointed warts, below the top the walls are often slightly folded; to 12 cm high, 4-8 cm in diameter.
Habitat & distribution: Singly or in groups, predominantly in coniferous forests occasionally in deciduous woodland and meadows; wide distribution, but much more rare than *Lycoperdon perlatum* (355) and *L. pyriforme* (356).

361 *Lycoperdon echinatum* ☠ Spiny Puffball

Fruit body: Spherical, somewhat flattened; dark brown and densely covered with long, pointed warts which fall off later starting from the middle, allowing the inner grey-black cover with a net-like pattern to be seen; to 4 cm in diameter, and approximately as high.
Gleba: White at first, later dirty purplish-brown, disintegrating with maturity.
Habitat & distribution: In deciduous woodland, mainly below beech often among leaf litter, therefore easily overlooked; rather frequent.

358

left
359

right
360

361

362 *Scleroderma citrinum* ☠ Common Earthball

Fruit body: Tuberous, club-like or spherical. Similar to a potato in form and weight; with light yellowish-brown, coarse, warty, net-patterned and very thick external skin; with thick, root-like fibres at the base; up to 10 cm in diameter.
Gleba: Inside the thick, white, outer layer purple-grey splashed with deep purple to olive-black, then disintegrating into flakes resembling cotton wool, always marbled with white.
Habitat & distribution: In coniferous forests and fens only on chalk-free soils; locally frequent. Consuming large amounts of this weakly poisonous fungus causes fainting spells and very strong gastric complaints. It is occasionally mixed with truffles as an adulteration.
Similar species: The inedible, softer and lighter *Scleroderma verrucosum*. It has at its base a conspicuous root-like structure of yellowish-white mycelium. It is more rare than *S. citrinum*.

363 *Rhizopogon obtextus* ☠

Fruit body: Tuber-like, usually half underground and densely covered with loose, root-like hyphae; yellowish-white and flaky at first, later yellowish-brown to light olive, up to 6 cm in diameter.
Gleba: Below a rather tough outer layer, at first yellowish-white, then yellowish and olive when mature; partitioned into small, irregularly deformed chambers, the white walls of which are clearly visible when the fungus is fully ripe.
Habitat & distribution: In sandy pine forests, usually half below the soil; rather rare.
Rhizopogon obtextus and *R. roseolus* (364), false truffles, are members of the Basidiomycetes. In spite of their subterranean habitat they are in no way related to the true truffles which belong to the Ascomycetes, the cup and flask fungi. True truffles that are famous as delicacies are *Choiromyces maeandriformis* and *Tuber brumale*, the winter truffle which occurs in Mediterranean regions. The morels (genus *Marchella*, see 381, p. 216) are other representatives of the Ascomycetes.

364 *Rhizopogon roseolus*

Fruit body: Tuberous to spherical; off-white at first, later dirty brown-red, marbled, turning red when touched; often covered in brownish, root-like hyphae; to 5 cm in diameter, but usually smaller.
Gleba: Off-white at first, slowly reddening when cut, later yellowish- to reddish-brown, dirty olive and disintegrating when old; it is divided into small chambers below the rather thick and firm outer cover.
Habitat & distribution: On bare soil in pine forests, but also among rubble in river meadows or on forest paths or roads, usually entirely above ground; rather frequent.

362

363

364

365 *Geastrum rufescens* ☠ Rosy Earthstar

Fruit body: At first half subterranean and surrounded by a spherical outer cover which later opens out and lifts up the spore-sac. In this process the outer cover, which grows to 10 cm in diameter, spreads flat. It tears, starting at the margin, into 7-10 regular lobes or rays which form a star. The spore-sac is spherical or a little flattened and fixed to the outer cover by a very short stem (this may also be absent). The spore-sac is light grey and has a small, toothed opening through which the ripe spores can escape.
Habitat & distribution: In deciduous and coniferous forests, occasionally in pastures; rather rare.
Similar species: The rare *Geastrum triplex* or collared earthstar which grows in groups among leaf litter under beech especially on chalky soil is similar, and one of the largest and most common earthstars. Its fruit body is up to 6 cm in diameter, gleba yellowish to greyish-brown. The spherical spore-sac is surrounded by an approximately 3 mm thick fringe-like layer which separates the spore-sac from the external cover. In coniferous forests grows *Geastrum coronatum*. This small earth star is common. It has a vertically upright outer cover, usually of four parts, and a grey-blue inner cover which is little more than 1 cm wide. The pointed conical opening of the latter is surrounded by a circular space. The tips of the external cover, which remain in the ground, are attached to a leather-like skin.

366 *Geastrum fimbriatum*

Fruit body: Initially spherical and growing underground. Its outer cover, which is greyish-white and 1-2 mm thick, eventually opens, tearing from the margin and dividing into up to 15 triangular lobes. During this process the fungus is raised above the ground and lies, in a typical star shape, loosely on the surface. The lobes roll back even more when the fungus is old. Open, the fungus reveals its spherical spore-sac. In it develops an at first white spore mass which discolours with age and becomes a greyish-brown spore dust. At the apex of the spore-sac is a fringed, warty opening serving for spore dispersal.
Habitat & distribution: In small groups in coniferous forests, mainly beside paths; rather frequent.
The earth stars are among the most curious organisms in nature. Of the species known in Europe most are fairly rare. Because they have a tough texture and centre which disintegrates to spore dust, they are not eaten; they are, however, not poisonous.

365

366

367 *Cyathus striatus* ☠ Bird's Nest Fungus

Fruit body: Shaped like an inverted cone when young; dark red-brown, with a very bristly surface which is leathery and tough; covered with a white skin before maturity; when skin tears it reveals the brownish-grey 'nest' part of the fungus with several egg-shaped peridioles (spore containers); 1-1.5 cm in diameter.
Habitat & distribution: On decaying wood among leaf litter on forest floors; frequent.

368 *Tulostoma brumale* ☠☒

Fruit body: Spherical with a long stalk, light straw-coloured when young, later pale ochre; with minute scales, and a narrow, downward directed ring at the point of stem insertion; a pointed opening arises from a brownish-black zone at the top; to 1.2 cm in diameter.
Stem: Pale grey; somewhat scaly, hollow and with small tubers at its base; up to 6 cm long and 3 mm in diameter.
Habitat & distribution: Mostly in autumn and winter, in dry and sunny spots; rare and should be protected.

369 *Astraeus hygrometricus* ☠

Fruit body: Subterranean when young, lying loose on the ground after unfolding its star-shaped external cover; whitish- to greyish-brown with spherical spore-sac. In dry weather the outer star points (or rays) roll up and cover the spore-filled sac; only to swell in the wet and spread out once more. This process can be repeated many times.
Habitat & distribution: Mostly under pines; in central and southern Europe, rare north of the Alps.

370 *Phallus impudicus* ☠ Common Stinkhorn

Fruit body: Semi-subterranean and egg-shaped when young, consisting of a hard, white kernel which is surrounded by a thick, transparent, jelly-like layer with a grey outer cover. After the 'witch's egg' has ruptured, a white shaft with a net-like, wrinkled surface appears and extends quickly. The cap is bell-shaped; on its honey comb patterned surface develops a slimy-sticky, olive-green spore mass which smells unpleasantly of carrion.
Habitat & distribution: In deciduous woodlands and coniferous forests; rather frequent; only the young 'witch's egg' is edible.

371 *Clathrus archeri* ☠

Fruit body: Resembling a squid. Enclosed in a whitish-grey cover when young; the arms, connected by their tips at first, emerge from this cover and spread after detaching from one another. The inside is filled by an olive-brown spore mass smelling of carrion.
Habitat & distribution: The fungus is from south east Asia and was introduced into Europe about 40 years ago, it can be observed in beech woodlands and parks.

left
367
right
368
369
left
370
right
371

372 *Auricularia auricula-judae* Jew's Ear

Fruit body: Bowl-shaped when young, later irregularly lobed, connected to the wood by a short stalk, inner surface dark greyish-brown to purple-black, folded along nerves, outer surface grey, rough and grainy; soft and jelly-like when moist, shrinking severely when dry; 4-10 cm in diameter.
Habitat & distribution: Throughout the year, particularly in winter and spring, in groups on dead elderberry, more rarely also on other species of wood.
This strongly swelling fungus has no taste, but is used in east Asian cookery. In the west it is known as Chinese morel. It is not related to the morels (genus *Marchella*) and does not look or taste like these fungi.

373 *Auricularia mesenterica* ☠ Tripe Fungus

Fruit body: Soft and jelly-like, somewhat leathery, dry, hard and shrinking, protruding horizontally; cap flaring and coarsely hairy at the edge, zoned light and dark greyish-brown; underside grey to purple brown; folded, ribbed and pruinose.
Habitat & distribution: Sometimes in large meadows; almost throughout the year, but mainly in late autumn and winter; on living wood of deciduous trees and still growing for a long time on dead trunks and stumps; not frequent.

374 *Exidia glandulosa* ☠ Black Witch's Butter

Fruit body: Inverted cone- to disc-shaped or hemispherical; completely black; fruit layer smooth above when young, later rough and minutely netted; densely covered with small, conical warts on the outside, folded a little near where fungus is in contact with host; soft and rubbery like jelly when moist; can resurrect after drying; up to 8 cm in diameter.
Habitat & distribution: Predominantly in winter on old oaks and lime trees, occasionally on other deciduous trees; fairly rare.

375 *Exidia recisa*

Fruit body: Inverted cone-shaped, often folded around contact area with host, soft and jelly-like; first yellowish-brown, dark red-brown when old, black when dried up; to 2 cm broad and high.
Habitat & distribution: Often in large colonies, mainly in winter, on dead branches of willow, more rarely on other deciduous trees; usually frequent in river meadows.

376 *Exidia plana* ☠

Fruit body: At first grey, spherical or disc-shaped, later folded like a brain; with minutely dotted surface, dark greyish-brown turning black; soft, transparent and jelly-like when moist, hard and crusty when dry.
Habitat & distribution: Often in extended lawns, mainly in winter and spring on deciduous wood, mainly on the cutting face of stored trunks or logs; frequent.

left 372

right 373

374

left 375

right 376

377 *Tremella mesenterica* ☠ Yellow Brain Fungus

Fruit body: Emerging as small nodules from tree bark when young, later folded irregularly like a brain; bright golden yellow, sometimes white and pruinose when young; soft like jelly and becoming a shapeless mess when old; up to 5 cm high and just as wide.
Habitat & distribution: Mainly in winter on dead branches of deciduous trees, predominantly in copses; rather frequent.
Similar species: Dacrymyces palmatus forms similar jelly-like fruit bodies, also coloured golden- to orange-yellow. Specific to conifer wood, it grows mainly at higher altitudes and is far more rare.

378 *Tremiscus helvelloides* ☺

Fruit body: Irregularly spathulate to funnel-shaped; bright orange, usually with a pink hue; soft and jelly-like; to 6 cm high, mostly 2-4 cm in diameter.
Habitat & distribution: Usually in large groups, on dead, decaying wood, also on the ground; prefers fringes of paths in coniferous forests; frequent at higher altitudes.
Due to its characteristic appearance *Tremiscus helvelloides* cannot be confused with any other fungus; it has no taste but is edible even when raw and can be prepared as a salad.

379 *Pseudohydnum gelatinosum* ☠ Jelly Tongue

Cap: Shell-shaped, with stalk to one side; white to dark greyish-brown with small nodules; soft like jelly; to 5 cm in diameter. Spines on the underside of cap are pure white, evenly pointed, to 3 mm long; flexible.
Flesh: First white, turning grey later; jelly-like, without taste or smell.
Habitat & distribution: On conifer stumps in late decay, mainly in moist and shady places, predominantly at higher altitudes. In spite of its spiny fruit layer, this fungus is one of the jelly fungi and has no connection to the true teeth fungi.

380 *Dacryomyces stillatus* ☠ Orange Jelly

Fruit body: Spotted or irregularly folded, often confluent with neighbouring fruit bodies; bright golden yellow to orange; 2-3 mm in diameter.
Flesh: Soft and jelly-like, very moist, without taste or scent.
Habitat & distribution: Often forming extended lawns, mainly at the cutting surface of stumps from deciduous or coniferous trees, also on the surface of felled, debarked trees; frequent.
The orange jelly forms two different kinds of fruit body. The incompletely developed state is spherical with a smooth surface; it appears as small orange-yellow spots (punct) which later flow apart. The fully developed fruit body is larger, often with folds or furrows and a paler yellow. Often both forms can be seen beside one another.

377

left
378
right
379

380

381 *Morchella esculenta* ☺ Common Morel

Cap: Irregularly spherical, egg-shaped or conical; ochre-yellow to honey-coloured, more rarely dark grey-brown; partitioned on the surface by broad, blunt ridges into many round, polygonal chambers: the smooth fruit layer lines their inside; hollow at the core; to 6 cm high and wide.
Stem: White; irregularly contorted, often rather flattened, with bulbous base, somewhat furrowed, hollow, minutely floccose or bare; up to 6 cm long and 2-3 cm thick.
Habitat & distribution: From March to May in groups, in gardens, parks, water meadows and in moist, deciduous woodland; not rare.
Use: Suitable for all recipes and for drying; improves soups and sauces.
Similar species: There is a danger of confusing the common morel with the very poisonous turban fungus *Gyromitra esculenta* (384).

382 *Morchella conica* ☺

Cap: Slim and conical with blunt apex; dark grey to chestnut-brown, more rarely ochre-grey; margin fused with stem; separated into elongated rhombic to almost square chambers by uninterrupted vertical ribs and irregular horizontal broad and blunt ridges; up to 6 cm, giant forms occasionally grow to 50 cm high and 3-4 cm wide.
Stem: White to pale ochre; thick or irregularly squashed or bent; at base a little wrinkly, minutely floccose and scaly, hollow.
Flesh: White to pale ochre; flexible, without scent, mild taste.
Habitat & distribution: April to June in deciduous and coniferous forests, mainly on piles of bark and at the side of forest roads, also on sites where there have been fires; rather frequent.
Similar species: Morchella conica has many forms and is split by some mycologists into several species, although these are probably only different habitat-based varieties. The tall morel *Morchella elata* has a lighter, red-brown cap and sometimes grows to more than half a metre. It grows in pine forests or on refuse sites and is rare.

383 *Mitrophora semilibera* ☺

Cap: Bell- or cap-shaped with a flared margin and blunt apex; ochre-brown, also red- to grey-brown, with vertical blunt ridges; to 3 cm wide and high.
Stem: White; evenly thick with a bulbous base, rather long, minutely scaly; base and apex often furrowed, hollow.
Flesh: White; waxy and brittle with weak scent and taste.
Habitat & distribution: April and May in large groups in moist deciduous forests, parks and river meadows; rather frequent.
Similar species: Ptychoverpa bohemica has a bell shaped cap, it is also bell-shaped and irregularly wrinkled. It grows in the same season in light deciduous woodlands and is very rare.

381

382

383

384 *Gyromitra esculenta* ☠ Turban Fungus

Cap: Spherical, irregularly lobed or contorted, brain-like, dark ochre- to red-brown; at insertion of stem there are usually reflexed lobes fused with the stem; 3-8 cm wide and just as high.
Stem: White; irregular; apex and base usually swollen and often flattened; with long folds or depressions; the interior is hollow and chambered.
Flesh: White; brittle with pleasant smell and taste.
Habitat & distribution: From April to May in large groups in sandy pine forests; very frequent in eastern Europe, otherwise rather rare.
The turban fungus contains gyromitrin, a deadly poison which is retained in the cooking process, its action is similar to that of α–amanitin. The poison evaporates after some time so that dried fungi are harmless. This fungus was till recently sold in markets in Europe and used a lot in the canning industry, but its sale is now prohibited. *Gyromitra esculenta* is wrongly described as edible if cooked in some fungus books, but it must not be eaten at all.

385 *Gyromitra infula* ☠ ☒

Cap: Irregularly folded and extending into two, rarely three or four bag-like, upward pointing appendages which grow in the shape of a mitre; dark cinnamon or red-brown; to 8 cm broad and high.
Stem: White; evenly thick, frequently flattened; firm when young with swollen apex; somewhat folded at the base and usually attenuated; firm when young, becoming hollow and chambered later.
Flesh: White; flexible, without scent, mild taste.
Habitat & distribution: In coniferous forests, mostly singly on stumps or around decaying wood, predominates at higher altitudes; fairly rare.
Gyromitra infula is regarded as edible, but should not be collected because of its rarity. It is not entirely certain that it contains gyromitrin, the poison of the saddle fungi. These fungi were formerly included in the genus *Helvella*, but are now distributed over several genera. This is due to their differing appearance, but also because of microscopic differences. They are distinguished from the morels, their closest relatives, by a fruit layer which is smooth or folded, but never chambered.

384

385

386 *Gyromitra gigas* ☠ ☒

Cap: Twisted in irregular wavy folds with lobes flat against or fused with the stem; ochre to reddish brown; to 20 cm high and wide.
Stem: White or pale ochre; thick and rather short, narrowed towards the base, rarely weakly bulbous, furrowed in folds, with smooth surface; internally hollow and chambered.
Flesh: White; mild taste and no scent, waxy, very brittle.
Habitat & distribution: From March to April in coniferous highland forests, on or around old stumps; rather rare and should be protected.
Gyromitra gigas is presumed not to be poisonous, but due to its great resemblance to *G. esculenta* (384) its consumption is not advised.

387 *Helvella elastica* ☠ Elastic Saddle

Cap: Divided into usually two or three flaring lobes, inrolled at the margin and saddle-like due to the lowered centre; whitish-grey, pale ochre to greyish-brown, rather tough, cartilaginous; up to 4 cm high and equally wide.
Stem: White or pale ochre; slender with a somewhat swollen base, often contorted, cartilaginous, flattened at the apex and minutely downy, hollow.
Flesh: Tough and without scent.
Habitat & distribution: Mainly along waysides among grass in deciduous and coniferous forests; mostly frequent.

388 *Helvella macropus* ☠

Cap: Irregularly shaped like a potato crisp when young, soon contorted and shaped like a broad bowl; fruit layer greyish-brown and smooth on the inside, with lighter greyish-white flocci on the outside, often tearing at the margin when old; up to 3 cm in diameter.
Stem: Whitish-grey, felty; often irregular, flattened, hollow when old.
Flesh: White; without taste or scent.
Habitat & distribution: In small groups on moist soil and among herbs in deciduous woodland, rarely also on decaying wood; rather frequent.
Similar species: Helvella corium has a shiny black fruit layer grows in early summer, but is far more rare.

389 *Helvella crispa* ☠ Common White Saddle

Cap: Of irregular shape with two to three vertical or flared lobes which are split at the rim; their underside is minutely velvety; upper surface is wrinkly or wavy; whitish-grey, more rarely dirty greyish-ochre to light hazel-brown; to 5 cm wide and equally high.
Stem: White; usually deeply furrowed with sharp-edged, longitudinal ribs with many horizontal cross connections; up to 6 cm long and 4 cm thick.
Flesh: White; quite brittle in the cap, elastic and tough in the stalk; without taste or smell.
Habitat & distribution: In deciduous and mixed forests, mainly along forest paths or roads, also among moss.

386

left
387
right
388

389

390 *Otidea onotica* ☠ Lemon Peel Fungus

Fruit body: Ear-shaped, and split to the base, rooting slightly, white and felty; fruit layer bright orange to yellow; mealy on the outside; to 4 cm high, 3 cm in diameter.
Flesh: White; without scent, mild taste.
Habitat & distribution: Mostly in small groups in deciduous and coniferous forests; fairly rare.
Similar species: A series of similar fungi exists which are difficult to distinguish. The hare's ear *Otidea leporina* is recognized only by its colour: rusty-yellow at first, then cinnamon-brown. The rather rare *O. concinna* grows in beech woods, its fruit bodies are bright lemon-yellow, split on one side, inrolled and form dense patches.

391 *Sarcosphaera crassa* ☠

Fruit body: Subterranean when young, forming a hollow sphere which subsequently extends, starts tearing from the apex and becomes a star shape, and is finally flat, up to 15 cm in diameter; off-white on the outside when young, later dirty ochre-grey, the smooth fruit layer inside has a pale violet or dingy brown hue.
Flesh: White; brittle, without scent, mild taste.
Habitat & distribution: From May to June mostly in groups, in coniferous forests on chalk, mainly at higher altitudes, fairly rare elsewhere.
The consumption of this poisonous fungus leads to severe gastric problems. This is one of the largest cup fungi (pezizas) and cannot be confused with any other fungus. Other species of cup fungi are much smaller and can be found in all seasons, but particularly in late autumn and spring on moist, decaying wood on the ground, on plant remains or on the soil. Many species are bright yellow, orange or red.

392 *Rutstroemia bulgarioides* ☠

Fruit body: Bowl-shaped when young, later flat and expanded; dark brown to almost black, always with a short little stalk which emerges from a cone scale (see photograph opposite) which is black at this point; mostly 3-6 mm, rarely to 1.5 cm in diameter.
Habitat & distribution: In dense masses, exclusively on moist pine cones on the ground; in coniferous highland forests, locally frequent after snow has melted.
Similar species: Ciboria rufofusa can be observed in April and May on the cone scales of silver fir when they have separated and lie moist on the ground. Its fruit bodies are light red to orange-brown, at first cup-shaped, later bowl-shaped or flat; to 1 cm in diameter. Also in spring *Ciboria amentacea*, the long-stalked alder cup fungus, grows on last season's alder catkins which have been covered by soil. Its fruit bodies are cup-shaped when young and later flat; they are ochre-brown, bearing minute marginal fungal threads.

390

391

392

393 *Peziza succosa* ☠

Fruit body: Rounded to oval, bowl-shaped with an irregular margin, stalkless; dark hazel-brown, outside lighter and minutely flaky; up to 6 cm, rarely 10 cm in diameter.
Flesh: Rather firm, immediately exudes a yellow sap when damaged.
Habitat & distribution: Mostly in small groups, in deciduous and coniferous forests, on bare soil; widely distributed.
Similar species: There are numerous species of cup fungi with similar colouration; the illustrated species can be easily recognized by its milk sap which turns yellow. The fruit layer of cup fungi is on the inside of the fruit body. The microscopically small asci (sacs) burst at maturity and release the spores. If one suddenly exposes cup fungi to the sun, the temperature stimulant will trigger a visible spore 'explosion'.

394 *Sarcoscypha austriaca* ☠ ☒

Fruit body: Cup-shaped with a short stem when young, later broad bowl-shaped with long inrolled, sometimes weakly notched margin; fruit layer bright cinnabar-red on the inside, outside light ochre or pink with white pustules; mostly 2-5 cm in diameter.
Habitat & distribution: In spring to May in small groups in moist, deciduous forests on dislodged pieces of wood on the ground, mainly in river meadows; fairly rare, should be protected.
Similar species: Caloscypha fulgens is similar in shape and size, but its fruit layer is bright orange and the outside is ochre-grey and grainy. *C. fulgens* grows after the snow has melted in coniferous mountain forests, rarely also among deciduous trees.

395 *Sowerbyella unicolor* ☠ ☒

Fruit body: Bowl-shaped when young, later flat with an irregular rim, bent up or downward; inside bright orange yellow, outside paler cream-coloured, minutely flaky; with a long rooting, white felty stem at the centre; up to 4 cm in diameter.
Habitat & distribution: Mostly in small and dense groups; in autumn in coniferous forests; very rare and should be protected.
Similar species: The even rarer *Sowerbyella radiculata* has a dark greyish, fibrous stem. It can safely be distinguished only on microscopic details. On dead wood of green alder and hornbeam grows the smaller *Rutstroemia bolaris*, up to 1 cm in diameter. Apart from size and habitat it is distinguished by its shorter stem and by growing in the summer.

393
394
395

396 *Ciboria batschiana* ☠

Fruit body: Plate-shaped when young, soon spread flat, dark grey-brown; smooth inside; up to 1.5 cm in diameter.
Stem: Mostly short, but can be several centimetres long, deeply rooted, contorted, black, smooth broadened at the apex.
Habitat & distribution: Sometimes in large numbers, exclusively on old acorns, which are mummified by the fungus and transformed into black lumps; rare.
Similar species: The tough *Rutstroemia firma* is similar but grows on the oak wood, mostly on fallen twiglets. The deep chestnut-brown *Sclerotinia tuberosa* grows in spring; its fruit bodies are at first cup-shaped, spread flat later, to 2 cm wide. It grows exclusively on the underground stem of the wood anemone, to which it is connected by a
10 cm long stem. The wood anemone does not die from this infestation but ceases flowering; there are several other long-stemmed species of a similar colour. The supporting substrate is of great importance for their identification.

397 *Chlorosplenium aeruginascens* ☠ Green Wood Cup

Fruit body: At first with a short stem and cup-shaped, then bowl-shaped, spreading to become entirely flat when old, then usually irregularly contorted; blue-green inside and smooth, outside almost white at first, later blue-green and a little flaky, to 1.5 cm in diameter.
Habitat & distribution: In groups on very decayed, debarked oak wood, occasionally also on wood of other deciduous trees; rare. The wood is stained green by the hyphae so the fungus can be detected even without fruiting.
Similar species: The green wood cup has recently been split into two species which are very similar and can only be distinguished using a microscope.

398 *Aleuria aurantia* ☠ Orange Peel Fungus

Fruit body: Bowl-shaped when young, can be spread flat later, irregularly contorted or torn, forming lobes; with bright orange-red fruit layer on the inside; light cream-pink and minutely flaky outside; mostly 2-3 cm, rarely up to 10 cm in diameter.
Habitat & distribution: Often in great numbers, fused in clumps on bare humus soil, sometimes also among stone debris on freshly prepared forest roads; not rare.
Similar species: Caloscypha fulgens has a more orange-yellow fruit body, its outside is grey when young, later orange and minutely granular. It grows in spring in coniferous highland forests. There are further brightly orange-coloured, but smaller cup fungi. Many of these are rare and require exact microscopic investigation to be identified.

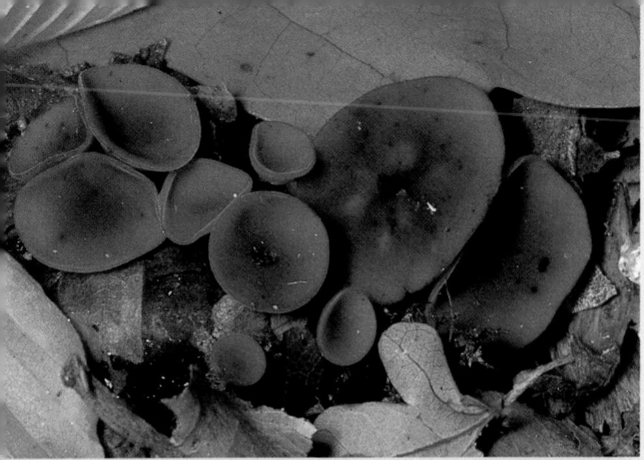

396

397

398

399 *Encoelia furfuracea* ☠

Fruit body: When young it forms a closed, hollow sphere with a cinnamon-brown, flaky outer wall; later it tears apart and spreads, star-shaped, revealing the smooth, light cinnamon- to red-brown fruit layer; up to 1.5 cm in diameter.
Habitat & distribution: In winter bursting from bark of newly dead, but standing, alder or hazel trunks, mostly in small and dense groups, which remain sound for weeks and survive even severe frosts; regarded as quite rare, but is probably often overlooked.
Similar species: The rare *Ionomidotis fulvotingens* also grows in winter on branches of hazel, alder and sycamore. Its fruit bodies grow in dense clumps, they are smaller and dark red-brown to almost black. They are cup-shaped when young, later flat and irregularly contorted. A further, almost black species of this genus, the very rare *Encoelia fascicularis*, is found in spring on branches of poplar and ash which lie on the ground but still retain their bark.

400 *Ascocoryne cylichnium* ☠

Fruit body: Soft and jelly-like, light red-violet to dirty brownish-lilac; occurs in two different forms. The completely developed fruit bodies (to the left in the picture opposite) are plate-shaped when young, when old they are evenly convex and circular with a short, attenuated stalk. They form sexual spores on their surface. Incomplete fruit bodies, referred to as the conidia stage (to the right), are irregularly lobed and fused with the neighbouring fruit bodies to produce a brain-like contorted mess. The spores of this fruit are formed in an asexual manner and differ from those of the fully developed fruit body. Often both forms are found side by side.
Habitat & distribution: Mainly in autumn and winter, on debarked deciduous wood, often on the cut surface of beech stumps; rather frequent.

401 *Bulgaria inquinans* ☠

Fruit body: At first conical, its outer skin dark brown and flaky, later bursting at the apex, revealing the black, moist and shimmering fruit layer.
Flesh: Brownish; like watery jelly, when dried rather hard, leathery and flexible.
Habitat & distribution: From October to March, mostly in groups on the bark of dead branches and felled oak trunks, more rarely on sweet chestnut, hornbeam and elm.
Similar species: Exidia plana (376) can look similar. If in doubt, run a finger over the fruit layer. A black staining is proof of identification for *B. inquinans*.

399
400
401

402 *Bisporella citrina* ☠

Fruit body: Circular, flat or weakly concave, without stalk or with only a very short one; bright lemon yellow; up to 3 mm in diameter.
Habitat & distribution: From autumn to spring, often in large, connected lawns on moist, felled and debarked deciduous wood, also on the cut surface of stumps; very frequent.
Similar species: The cup-shaped *Hymenoscyphus calyculus* is very similar, but somewhat larger, its stalk is up to 4 mm long. It grows from October on wood debris. A microscope is required to identify both species accurately as they are distinguished by the shape of their spores.

403 *Nectria coccinea* ☠

Fruit body: Rounded or somewhat pear-shaped, with smooth surface and a small wart at the apex; tiny, to only 0.5 mm in diameter.
Habitat & distribution: On the wood of various deciduous trees, particularly on maple, mostly in small colonies, bursting from the bark, also singly on debarked wood, observed almost throughout the year; frequent.
Similar species: Nectria episphaeria is even smaller and grows singly. The fungus can be recognized only through a lens; it grows throughout the year on the hard, black surface of various wood-encrusting fungi (see various species of *Stereum* (321)) that grow on dead, deciduous trees. There are numerous other *Nectria* species.

404 *Nectria cinnabarina* ☠ Coral Spot Fungus

Fruit body: Occurring in two different forms: the fertile form consists of a small pile of tiny, cinnabar-red globules with a small wart at the apex; they are up to 1.5 mm wide. The imperfect form is larger, pink, smooth and up to 2 mm wide. Not infrequently both stages are found beside one another, making it possible to observe how the perfect fungi gradually develop. The imperfect stage is present in many ascomycetes with a simple construction. It is so different from the perfect stage that they have even been described as separate species.
Habitat & distribution: In late autumn and winter on deciduous trees; in large numbers on dead twigs that have retained their bark; often both forms are seen together; very frequent.

405 *Geopyxis carbonaria* ☠

Fruit body: Cup-shaped, usually evenly circular; white and mealy towards margin on the outside; dark red-brown, with a light white-notched rim; up to 2 cm in diameter.
Stem: Same colour as the fruit body; slender, deeply immersed in the soil.
Habitat & distribution: From April, exclusively on burnt soil; mostly in groups; not frequent.

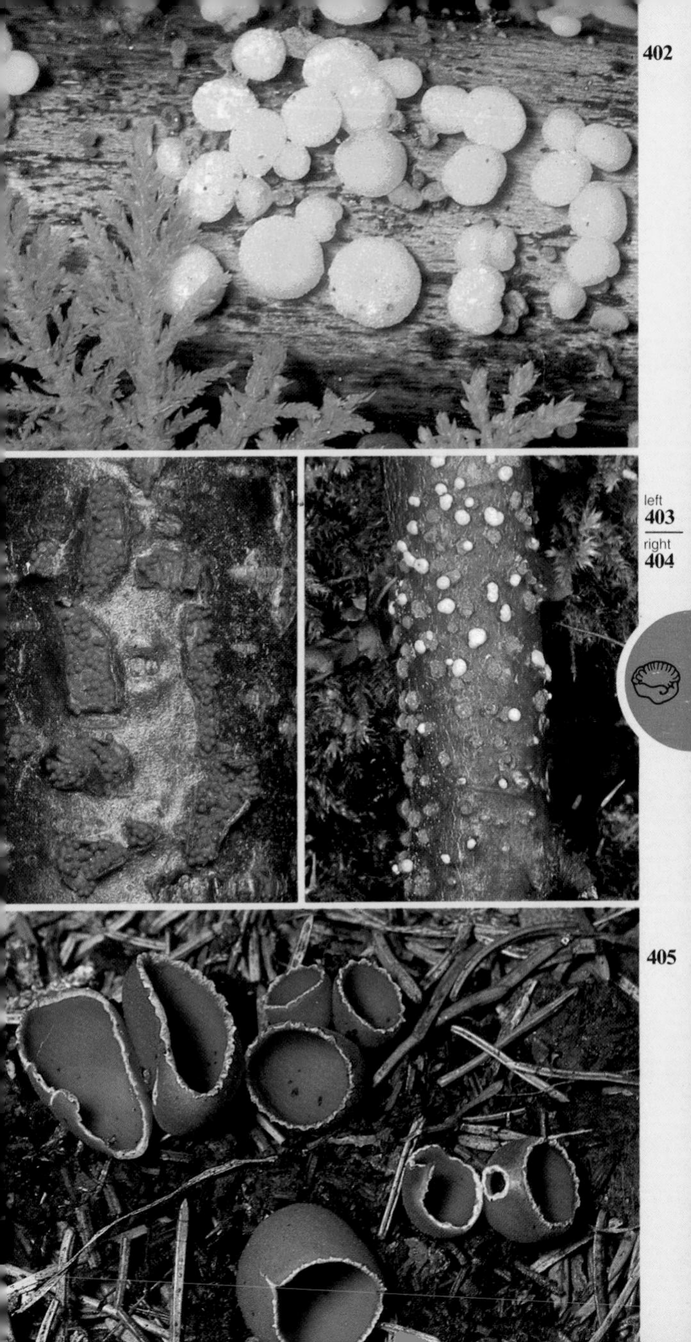

402
left
403
right
404
405

406 *Xylaria polymorpha* ☠ Dead Man's Fingers

Fruit body: Slender, club-shaped, often irregularly contorted and flattened at the apex; dark grey-brown when young, later completely black, dotted with minute warts apart from on the short indistinct stem; very hard and firm, up to 4 cm high, stem to 7 mm long, top to 1 cm wide.
Flesh: Below the black, crusty surface pure white; somewhat fibrous, without scent.
Habitat & distribution: Mostly in smaller groups, throughout the year at the base of old, mossy beech stumps, occasionally also on other deciduous wood; frequent.

407 *Xylaria hypoxylon* ☠

Stag's Horn Fungus or Candle Snuff Fungus

Fruit body: Branched antler-like, flat at the tip, very hard and firm, not breaking when bent; off-white and pruinose; up to 2 cm high.
Stem: Black at the base, whitish-grey towards the top.
Habitat & distribution: Almost throughout the year, but predominantly in autumn and winter on dead wood of deciduous trees, mostly on the cut surface of beech stumps, rarely on coniferous wood; very frequent.

408 *Cudonia circinnans* ☠

Cap: Rounded, flat, with tightly inrolled margin, usually depressed at the centre; pale ochre-red; up to 2 cm in diameter.
Stem: Same colour as the cap, sometimes reddish brown or pale lilac towards base; rather long, rounded or flattened; to 3 cm long and 5 mm thick.
Flesh: Firm, somewhat cartilaginous in cap, no scent, mild taste.
Habitat & distribution: In crowded fairy rings in grassy, coniferous highland forests; fairly rare.

409 *Leotia lubrica* Lizard Tuft or Jelly Babies

Cap: Spherical when young, later irregularly lobed; yellowish-ochre to light olive-brown; to 2 cm in diameter.
Stem: Mostly light yellow or ochre; minutely flaky.
Flesh: Watery, brownish; soft and jelly-like, no scent or taste.
Habitat & distribution: Mostly in moist woods between moss and grass, often in large groups, not rare.
Similar species: Leotia atrovirens occurs in hues from dark green to almost black. It grows at forest fringes and under deciduous trees, in moist places as well as at higher altitudes; very rare.

410 *Cordyceps ophioglossoides* ☠

Fruit body: Club- to tongue-shaped; top part round or flat, minutely warty; dirty greyish-yellow at the base, otherwise dark red-brown to black; very hard and tough; up to 4 cm high.
Habitat & distribution: Moist coniferous forests, parasitic on the underground truffle (*Elaphomyces*) and connected to it by bright yellow mycelium; locally frequent, but easily overlooked.

left
406
right
407
408
left
409
right
410

411 *Fuligo septica* ☠ Flowers of Tan

Fruit body: A slimy lemon-yellow organism without distinct form. When old, the foamy lumps become off-white, reddish or brownish and are encased by a calcium crust.
Habitat & distribution: In summer and autumn after rain on moss, on stumps and on leaf litter; very frequent everywhere.
This fungus belongs with the Myxomycetes (as do *Lycogala epidendrum* (412) and *Ceratiomyxa fruticulosa* (414)). These curious organisms exist at the border between plant and animal. They are a shapeless mass of protoplasm, which can even move its position on a given surface. Structurally they resemble unicellular animals like amoebae. Firm at maturity, they are distributed by spores.

412 *Lycogala epidendrum* ☠

Fruit body: Bright red, minutely warty, globular shapes, to 1.5 cm in diameter; at first soft and filled with a cinnabar-red mass, the plasmodium later discolour to grey-green or brown, firm. The skin of the mature fruit body dissolves, releasing the spores.
Habitat & distribution: On decayed stumps, mostly in small colonies, predominantly in summer after rain.
As all other Myxomycetes *Lycogala epidendrum* thrives on bacteria, fungal spores and various micro-organisms; the wooden support to which it is attached is not affected.

413 *Claviceps purpurea* ☠ Ergot

Fruit body: Blackish-purple, tube-like shapes which replace the cereal grain on mature ears. During the flowering season the spores of ergot affect the stigmata of various grasses, mainly barley and rye. When the pathologically changed, contaminated grains are mixed with the cereal during milling, the ergot poison in the flour, the ergotin, sparks off a life-threatening illness in humans. Ergotism was formerly widespread; it leads to the disturbance of the nervous system and brain function and can even lead to the atrophy of fingers and toes. Due to cleansing of cereal grain, ergot has become more rare. One should not underestimate the danger of an ergot poisoning when 'organically grown' flour is used.

414 *Ceratiomyxa fruticulosa* ☠

Fruit body: Very small, white, dainty branched and soft-spongy shapes.
Habitat & distribution: On old stumps mostly in crevices of wood or over moss; can form human palm-sized expanses; in summer very frequent after rain, but frequently overlooked; one of the most common slime-fungi.

411

left
412
right
413

414

A short synopsis of fungi

Fungi and their history

Although there are reports of edible and poisonous fungi dating back to ancient Rome, these plants were a puzzle to students of the natural sciences for a considerable time. Fungi were regarded as 'vapours' of moist soil, because they appeared suddenly without allowing observers to see where they originated from. Moreover, they produced no fruits or seeds and so did not fit into the framework created for the plant world by the early natural scientists. Therefore, it is no surprise that fungi were regarded as devilry, the work of dark powers.

The fungi only gained more esteem when the Italian scientist Peter Anton Micheli discovered fungal spores in 1710 and consequently found the key to fungal reproduction.

In about 1750 the great Swedish botanist Carl von Linnée (Linnaeus) designed a framework for the entire fauna and flora as it was then known, a system that allowed both to be surveyed and understood more easily. But even he, who coined many of the Latin animal and plant names still used today, had no real grasp of the classes of fungi. It was left to his compatriot Elias Fries to be the first scientist of natural history to penetrate more deeply into the secrets of fungi. His work 'Systema Mycologica', published in 1821, is still recognised as the foundation of fungal systematics (mycology). Mycology made giant steps in the 150 years that followed. More and more species were recognised and described, and at the same time new methods for distinguishing species were developed. We recognise today that an exact fungi identification is guaranteed only by using a microscope. In some particularly difficult groups, the identification has to be confirmed by tests for chemical reactions and even by the investigation of pigments.

The layperson may find limitations in his or her ability to identify fungi by just using pictures and short species descriptions. However, many fungus species can be safely identified without modern scientific methods if the external characteristics are checked out carefully.

What is a fungus?

The fungi which we find in woodland, meadows, fields or even flower pots are merely the fruit bodies of a plant living in concealment. In contrast to more sophisticated or highly evolved plants, fungi do not have chlorophyll and cannot therefore assimilate organic compounds. They break up remains of dead plant material and from these compose new organic substances which, in turn, serve as nutrients for other organisms.

In this way fungi fulfil the role of waste disposers in nature. Their work is not only environmentally friendly and clean (it leaves no residues) but they are natural recyclers, ensuring that everything that has run its course in nature can be used once more. Apart from a few bacteria, fungi are the only organisms which can decompose dead wood. Even the wood worm carries fungal cultures in its digestive tract which enable it to cope with its woody food.

But the role of fungi in nature does not end with this ingenious use of refuse. Many fungi combine with the roots of living plants, especially those of trees in forests. Here they proliferate on in what is called a *mycorrhiza*. If the fungal threads only surround the root mycorrhiza are known as *ektotrophic*. This is a relationship for mutual gain, a symbiosis, as the fungus obtains nutrients from the tree root and, in turn, supplies water and salts to its host. Many species of fungi enjoy symbiotic relationships with other plants, for almost all boletes and for all fungi with a veil (cortina), for instance, this symbiosis is a matter of survival. There is also evidence that trees, growing without a mycorrhizal partner, prosper less well. In nature such symbioses are already functional in young plants. Orchids, for example, rely so much on a fungal partner that they cannot even germinate in its absence.

When and where do fungi grow?

Fungi appear predominantly in late summer and autumn and require a good level of moisture to be able to grow. One thunder storm after a prolonged dry period is not enough, however, to let fungi 'mushroom' from the soil overnight. Species have specific needs but usually require a preparation time of 2–10 days to form a fruit body. As soon as the first fruit bodies appear, further development proceeds rather quickly, often in the space of a few hours. This is particularly true for the smaller species, while the large polypores need, as a rule, a few days for completion. The amanitas (152, 153, 154) are an exception. After splitting or tearing the volva they only need to extend their stems and expand the cap. In some freshly harvested fungi one can observe how the fruit body develops fully during a few hours if left in a warm room.

In suitable weather fruit bodies of firm-fleshed species remain in good condition for many weeks if they are not attacked by grubs of the many fungus flies. The hard, shelf-like fruit bodies of polypores can live for many years on wood and form a new fruit layer annually. If you notice how many fungus species can appear in the course of a few years in a small area, you will realise that some fungi recur seasonally; yet other species can seem to be absent for years and suddenly appear again. Different areas support different fungus species. Not only is the presence of different tree species important, but the type of soil as well. Some fungus species grow predominantly in old woods, others in forest nurseries.

The science involved with research into fungus habitats is fungus ecology. Unfortunately the needs of individual species is still not entirely known. It might be possible one day to create ideal 'penny-bun' conditions and to specifically foster the growth of these delicate edible fungi. At the moment we are only aware that an intense competition exists in the world of fungi and that only a winning species can bring its fruit bodies to full maturity. The results of this competition are usually determined by temperature, rain and soil type and even now man is not able to exert a directing influence on this course of nature. However, environmental conditions caused by forest misuse, air pollution and many other changes do affect the fungus flora.

How do fungi multiply?

The fungal spores, transported locally by air currents or carried by the wind, often over large distances, form a white *wheft* (cover of fungal threads) on suitable soils which is called the *uni-nucleate mycelium*. A precondition for the formation of new fruitbodies is the fusion of mycelia from two whefts of different lineage. In this process the cells unite, but the nuclei remain separate. Each cell of a wheft capable of fruiting and each cell of a fruit body thus has two nuclei, and a *heterothallic mycelium* has been formed. Only when spore formation is initiated in the basidium (see p. 243), do the two nuclei divide and subsequently form four new nuclei by immediate double division. This system of procreation applies to the majority of the **Basidiomycetes** (*Boletus*, *Russula* etc.); in the **Ascomycetes** (*Marchella*, *leziza* etc.) the principle is similar, but in the ascus (tube) usually eight spores are developed (see Kingdom of fungi p. 242). Particularly in species of a more primitive nature (those at a lower evolutionary stage), procreation is complicated by the formation of supplementary fruit forms which sometimes have a totally different external appearance.

The spore production of fungi reaches unimaginary scales. Gill fungi of a medium size shed between 25 and 40 million spores hourly. Even short-lived species can produce several billion spores by this system. One mature penny-bun produces over 10 billion spores in a fortnight. If every spore gave rise to just one penny-bun, a goods train with wagons over 500 km long could be filled. Anxieties that one could stop the shedding of spores by premature harvesting to such an extent that a species could become extinct, are probably untrue. It must be remembered that a mycelium can survive in the soil and form fruit bodies for centuries.

Fungi on Wood

Fungal species from a great variety of families grow on wood. The spores of these fungi are very aggressive and use every opportunity to penetrate the wood. Healthy trees can resist such attack because of their protective bark; dead trees and those weak from age or illness are much more likely to be infected. When the bark is damaged through breakage or cuts, ideal opportunities for fungal infections are created. Without leaving visible external traces, the mycelium penetrates deep into the heart wood. In this process certain fungal species decompose only the cellulose and lignin in the wood, leaving the carbohydrate content untouched. The wood then retains its structure for a long time, but turns a very light colour; this is the white rot to which the wood of deciduous trees fall prey. Conversely, fungi attacking coniferous trees often utilise only the carbohydrates in the wood. The wood then crumbles and becomes brown-red; this is termed brown rot. As soon as the first fruiting bodies appear on the stem, the heart wood is already largely destroyed and the tree cannot be saved.

The destruction of sick and weak trees by fungi in nature is necessary and never causes real damage. Only where man interferes with nature and does not plant trees which suit the locality or habitat, can a fungus become a dangerous destroyer. The honey fungus *Armillaria mellea* (178) and the root fomes *Heterobasidium annosum* (311), both of which can attack and destroy the majority of a population of firs of similar ages in a commercial forest, are prime examples of this. In naturally generated forests with trees of varying age the honey fungus never occurs on living trees. The root fomes even appears to be completely absent from areas where firs grow naturally.

Where fungi grow on dead trees or stumps, we can often observe a cornucopia of forms. If one studies the fungal growth on a trunk for some time, it can be seen that fungi appear in ranked order. Some species, the honey fungus for instance, grow on newly dead and still hard wood, whilst others, like the *Hericium coralloides* (343), appear only when the wood has crumbled extensively. In dry and sunny places fungi different from those that grow on stumps in the dense undergrowth will be observed. *Gloeophyllum sepiarium* (325) for instance, grows only on free stacked and dry wood whilst *Gloeophyllum odoratum* (319) always grows in moist and shady places.

Fairy Rings

Some species of fungi often establish rows or crescents which close up to form rings. The explanation for this rare natural phenomenon is quite simple. Some fungi grow in uniformly symmetrical places in all directions from their point of origin (in the centre) and form their fruit bodies in the zone where incremental additions are made by the living fungus. The fungi then appear in a circle that increases in size every year. If growth is interrupted, the circle dissolves into crescents or rows. The age of a ring can be judged from its speed of growth and its size which can measure several hundred metres in diameter; there are some fairy rings which have been recorded as up to 700 years old. Fairy rings are formed only by certain species of fungi. The penny-bun and the fly agaric, for instance, do not form fairy rings.

Poisonous fungi and fungal poisons

Since fungi were first used by humans, the poisonous nature of some of them has been recognised. From early on means have been explored to to find out whether a fungus contain poison or not, in order to avoid the danger some pose. The folkloric rules that have been established to this end are, unfortunately, wrong without exception. There is no general indicator for the recognition of poisonous fungi, only the mycological characteristics of every individual species can reveal whether or not it contains poison. The reason some fungi are so dangerous is that unlike any other living thing, fungi are able to assimilate extremely complicated organic compounds. Their chemical make up differs fundamentally from that of flowering plants. One group of fungi assimilates poisonous substances which attack human organs such as the liver, the kidneys and the blood circulation with potentially fatal consequences. The most dangerous of these fungal poisons are: **α-Amanitin** – This is the poison of the bulbous agarics (p. 82, p. 84, numbers 150 and 151 in particular). It was discovered also in *Galerina marginata* (one of the pixy caps – p. 100) and could, moreover, be contained in some of the smaller, mostly rare, lepiotas (p. 34). It leads to a destruction of the liver even in small quantities and is the most frequent cause of fungal poisoning.

Orellanin – This is found in *Cortinarius orellanus* and in *C. rubellus* (p. 122) and in some closely related species; it may also be contained in *Cortinarius splendens* and its close relatives (p. 130). Orellanin leads to protracted poisonings, often with permanent kidney damage. Consumption can often be fatal.

Gyromitrin – The poison of *Gyromitra esculenta*, the turban fungus (p. 218), was discovered only two decades ago; its acts similarly to α-amanitin.

Muscarin – This poisonous substance is contained in many species of fungus. It is present in life-threatening amounts only in some *Inocybe* (p. 104 and p. 120) and in poisonous *Clitocybe* (p. 36). Muscarin acts as a nerve poison and affects the heart and blood circulation; it can be neutralised by atropin from *Atropa belladonna*. Although it is contained in small doses in *Amanita pantherina* and *A. muscaria* the real danger posed by both these fungi is due to other poisonous substances.

In addition to these poisons there are many fungi which, although they contain no dangerous poisonous substances, can cause gastric problems involving several days of sickness. Not all fungus species have been investigated at this stage; for example *Paxillus involutus*, the brown roll-rim (247) was recognised as being dangerous only in 1972. We must urgently warn against attempts to taste unknown fungi.

Heavy metal content: It has been only recently discovered that some naturally growing fungi contain considerable amounts of the poisonous heavy metals lead, quick silver and, most of all, cadmium. The content is completely independent of the locality and is not limited to fungi growing in industrial areas. It is not necessary to avoid eating all metal-containing fungi, especially in view of the fact that other foods, particularly liver and kidney, contain much higher amounts of these than any fungus. However, a constant consumption of fungi should be avoided, particularly of the cadmium-rich Agaricus (p. 94) or the Macrolepiotas (p. 86).

How can we identify a gill or tube fungus?

Any given species can be identified by the appearance and nature of its fruit body. In each case a knowledge of the individual parts of that structure is required. Most species that are of interest for the fungus gatherer and nature-lover are built according to a uniform scheme. On top of a **stem**, which emerges from the ground, is a **cap**, inrolled when young and later spread; on its underside a fruit layer is formed, which consists of **gills** or **tubes**. The cap is usualy closed in the early stages of development and soon spreads to become hemispherical, and later convex to flat or funnel-shaped. (Forms of caps characteristic for many fungal species are illustrated on the inside of the back cover.) The cap surface is often coloured. It is covered by a skin (pellicle) that can be pulled off either in part or entirely in some species. The pellicle can be slippery, velvety, felty, scaly, smooth, matt or glossy. Occasionally one finds floccose or membranous, more rarely silky or fibrous remains of a cover or veil which envelops the young fruit body and tears as it grows. Not infrequently vestiges of this cover remain on the stem and on the bulbous base.

The **gills** of the various gill fungi can be narrow, broad, thick or thin. They can be decurrent (continuing deep down on the stem), but can also be sinuous or free (of the stem). Sometimes the gills branch in a fork-like manner; more often gills are shorter towards the rim of the cap. In some fungi the gills are connected at their base by cross veins. (All these characteristics are illustrated on the inside of the back cover.) The colour of the gills should be noted carefully, because they often change colour in the course of the fruit body's development. Gills of fungi of entirely different family groups can have the same colour at least at a young stage. The gill edge can be smooth, finely or coarsely denticulate (toothlike); it can also be minutely (slightly) floccose, exude small droplets of water and have a different colour from the main part or blade of the gill.

The **tubes**, which tube fungi have in the place of gills, are a spongy layer which can easily be separated from the flesh of the cap. They are usuallly grey or yellow when young and often turn olive when the spores ripen.

The openings on the underside are the **pores**. They can be narrow or wide and are coarsely dentate in some species. A few tube fungi have red pores.

During the development of the fruit body the **stem** can alter its appearance very much. (All important stem forms are illustrated on the inside of the front cover.) In many fungi the gills or tubes are initially covered by a second membrane which later remains as a ring or ring-like zone on the stem. The **flesh** can be various colours and show different discolourations when cut. It can be of various different textures in different species: soft like cotton wool, brittle and crumbly, tough, elastic or fibrous and exude a white or coloured milk sap (latex). The taste of the raw flesh or of the milk has only been given for fungi that are not poisonous. On its own the taste gives no indication of the edibility of the fungus. Tasting the raw flesh to prove the result of an identification must only be done when there is absolute certainty that the fungus is not poisonous.

The **habitat** or locality of a fungus is a valuable clue to its identification. Not only are the closest tree species important, but also the moisture and nature of the soil. Where fungi grow on wood, the type of wood (i.e. whether the tree is deciduous or coniferous) should be made note of.

The **smell** of a fungus is one of the most valuable clues in identifying species without a microscope. Some experience is required until one can distinguish the smells which tend to be particularly distinct on the squashed gills of fresh fungi. The spectrum of fungal scents extends from cocoa flakes, aniseed, gooseberry compote and bitter almonds, to radish, decaying cabbage, garlic and potatoes. The colour of **spores** is a very important factor in the identification of tube and gill fungi and has, therefore, been provided in their descriptions. Although important structural characteristics of spores require the use of a microscope with x1000 magnification, a 'spore print' can easily be easily made to establish their colour . A sound, mature fungal cap is laid on a white sheet. In an atmosphere free of air currents the spores fall between the tubes or gills on to the paper. The print may take minutes or hours to make.

Microscopic characteristics: Beyond details visible to the naked eye are the microscoic details which are a world of wonder to the fungus enthusiast. Colour, form and size of spores allow us not only to recognise various families and genera, they also reveal in their structure the tiniest works of living nature. Objects of further interest that provide identifying characteristics are the spore forming basidia and asci as well as the cystidia, between the fruiting cells. The collector who is well versed with dissecting techniques will investigate the layering and structure of the pellicle and gills. All such details have an important role in dividing fungi into families and genera but these tests cannot be made during a simple fungal foray, and only an experienced mycologist will be able to classify fungi while in the field.

Different forms of spores (magnification x 1000)

Different forms of cystidia (magnification x 500)

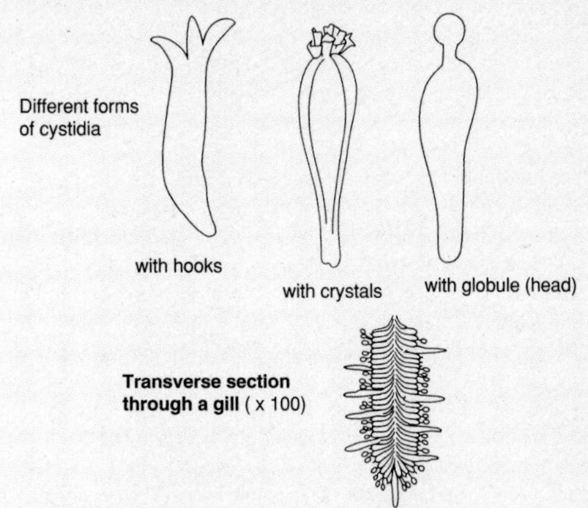

The kingdom of fungi

Just like the flowering plants, fungi are also arranged in **classes, orders, families, genera** and **species**. However, as the classification of fungi does not often follow external characteristics, it is sometimes almost impossible for the layperson to understand the way fungi are naturally related. The following 'family tree' was designed to show the most important fungal groups in spite of this. It does not delineate the latest scientific findings, but enables anyone recognise the relationship of the most important forms of fruit bodies.

Class: Cup fungi & flask fungi (Ascomycetes)

Spores ripen in spore-sacs (asci) usually containing 8 spores

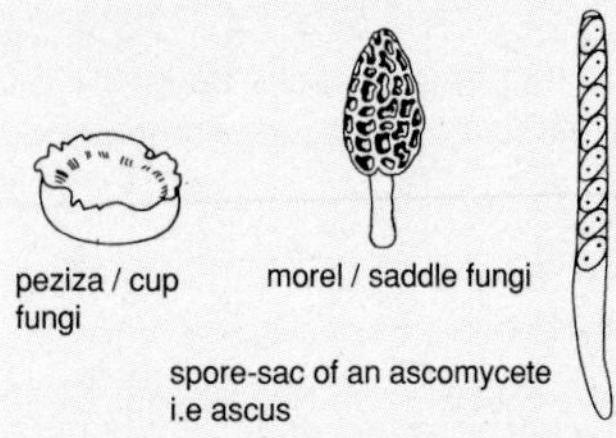

Class: palisade fungi (Basidiomycetes)
Spores, usually 4 at a time, ripen on basidia

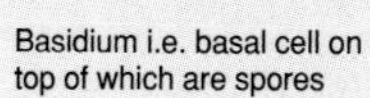

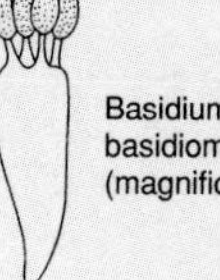

Fungi without gills

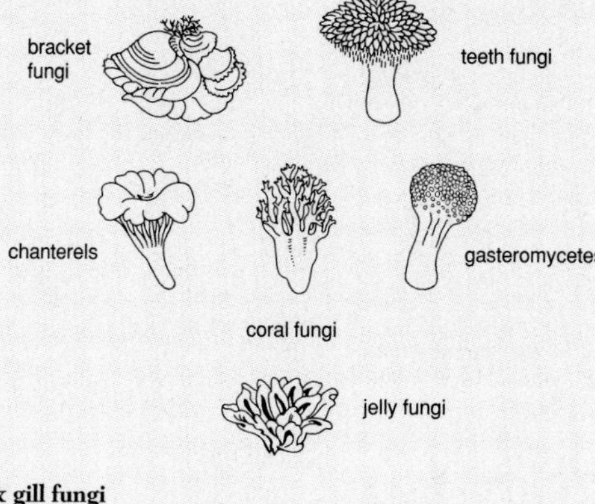

Tube & gill fungi

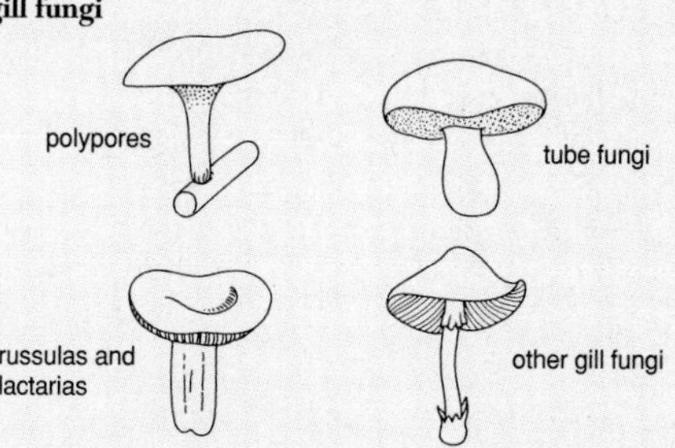

Fungal groups which are only of scientific interest, for example, the moulds which belong among the Ascomycetes or the smuts and rusts, have not been included. Apart from fungi with gills, present day fungal systematics is very complicated and subject to constant change.

The Cap fungi

The cap fungi, that is the tube fungi, gill fungi and some of the cap-forming polypores, make up the largest part of the fungal flora commonly seen. It is not easy to identify, by external characteristics alone, the approximately 2500 different species of fungi to their correct families and genera. The signs of natural relationships, as far as they are known with any certainty, can only be recognised under the microscope or proved through chemical analysis. The classification below can, therefore, give only a rough survey of the systematics of the cap fungi (as described and illustrated in this book). It includes only the most important genera and is limited to the species contained in this fungal guide. An attribution of unknown fungi to a family and genus will therefore not always be possible – it is not always easy for the specialist either.

ORDER: Polyporales, bracket fungi
Family: Polyporaceae
Fungi with tough flesh, fruit layer with pores or gills, stem often attached to wood on one side.
Genera: *Polyporus* (p. 28), *Pleurotus* (p. 32)

ORDER: Boletales, boletes and relatives
Family: Boletaceae, tube fungi
The fruit layer consists of a soft layer of tubes which can be detached. Spores mostly brown to olive in colour.
Genera: *Boletus* (p. 8-14,p. 18), *Xerocomus* (p. 16,18)
Tylopilus (p. 8), *Suillus* (p. 18-22)
Leccinum (p. 24), *Gyroporus* (p. 18)
Gyrodon (p. 14), *Boletinus* (p. 20)
Chalciporus (p. 18), *Pulveroboletus* (p. 18)
Family: Strobilomycetaceae
Distinguished from the Boletaceae mainly by diverging spore structures and pigments
Genera: *Strobilomyces* (p. 26), *Porphyrellus* (p. 26)
Family: Paxillaceae
Fruit layer consisting of low decurrent, frequently forked gills.
Genera: *Paxillus* (p. 140), *Hygrophoropsis* (p. 198)
Family: Gomphidiaceae
Fleshy fungi with distant, decurrent gills. Spores: olive-black
Genera: *Gomphidius* (p. 58), *Chroogomphus* (p. 142)

ORDER: Agaricales, gill fungi
Family: Hygrophoraceae
Gills mostly white, slightly thick and widely spaced; spore-forming basidia rather long
Genera: *Hygrophorus* (p. 54-58), *Hygrocybe* (p. 54)
Family: Tricholomataceae
Fungi of most variable form and size with white, pink or cream-coloured spores; with sinuous or decurrent white, yellow or, more seldom, cream or blue gills
Genera: *Omphalina* (p. 42), *Ricknella* (p. 40)
Laccaria (p. 34), *Clitocybe* (p. 36, 38, 62, 64)
Lepista (p. 60, 64, 66), *Tricholoma* (p. 68-72)
Tricholomopsis (p. 68), *Armillariella* (p. 100)
Lyophyllum (p. 36, 50), *Calocybe* (p. 64)
Asterophora (p. 52), *Pseudoclitocybe* (p. 50)
Melanoleuca (p. 74), *Catathelasma* (p. 98)
Collybia (p. 38, 46, 48, 76), *Marasmiellus* (p. 52)

Micromphale (p. 44, 52), *Panellus* (p. 32)
Oudemansiella (p. 74, 96), *Megacollybia* (p. 74)
Xerula (p. 74), *Strobilurus* (p. 42)
Marasmius (p. 44, 48, 52), *Macrcystidia* (p. 38)
Mycena (p. 40, 42, 52), *Xeromphalina* (p. 46), *Flammulina* (p. 46)
Family: Entolomataceae Fungi of various sizes, gills and spores pink, spores angular
Genera: *Rhodocybe* (p. 48), *Clitopilus* (p. 50), *Entoloma* (p. 40, 50, 60)
Family: Pluteaceae Gills as in Nos. 88 & 140, soft rose-pink, spores pink
Genera: *Pluteus* (p. 50, 74), *Volvariella* (p. 76)
Family: Amanitaceae Gills white, free, spores white, mostly with ring and universal veil Genera:
Amanita (p. 78-84), *Limacella* (p. 76)
Family Agaricaceae Gills white or brown, free, spores white or brown; cap often scaly, without universal veil, stem mostly with ring
Genera: *Agaricus* (p. 92-94), *Melanophyllum* (p. 110)
Cystolepiota (p. 34), *Lepiota* (p. 34, 88)
Macrolepiota (p. 86, 88), *Cystoderma* (p. 90), *Phaeolepiota* (p. 98)
Family Coprinaceae
Lamellae black, often dissolving, spores dark brown to black
Genera: *Coprinus* (p. 110, 112), *Panaeolus* (p. 110)
Panaeolina (p. 110), *Anellaria* (p. 96), *Psathyrella* (p. 112, 142)
Family Strophariaceae
Gills yellowish-brown, grey or dark brown, spores mostly dark brown, cap often slippery, spores smooth
Stropharia (p. 96, 110), *Hypholoma* (p. 102)
Pholiota (p. 114, 116), *Kuehneromyces* (p. 100)
Family Cortinariaceae
Gills when young white, pale clay, yellow, lilac, olive, rust- or dark brown with trichome veil; spores rust- to dark brown, spores often warty
Genera: *Inocybe* (p. 104, 120), *Hebeloma* (p. 118)
Gymnopilus (p. 102), *Dermocybe* (p. 108)
Cortinarius (p. 106, 122-138), *Rozites* (p. 98), *Galerina* (p. 40, 100)

ORDER: Russulales
Family: Russulaceae
Fibrous
Genera: *Russula* (p. 144-158), *Lactarius* (p. 158-174)

Are the fungi dying out?

It is a current concern that over collecting fungi could threaten their population or even cause some species to become extinct. However, in the past few years harvests of fungi have been particularly heavy in some areas. It is usually the interests of wood owners and foresters that are behind requests for the prohibition of fungi collecting. If the protection of fungi is nature conservation, then not only the effects of land owners have to be considered; to some extent the mushroom collectors are at fault as well. Often groups of city folk ramble through woods leaving behind them a trail of destruction, among which are dislodged and trampled fungi. It is no wonder that the more popular edible fungi have become a rarity in the vicinity of larger towns. Besides thoughtful behaviour in the field, careful collection without damaging the soil cover should be the top priority for every collector and nature lover. But to blame the fungus collector for the critical decrease in fungi population is to lose sight of the main problem.

Changes in the environment everywhere have increased the pressure particularly on rarer fungi. The destruction of old meadows, woods and fens mean that fungus species that require such habitats disappear as well. Where today are dead trees left standing just in order to grant survival for wood destroying fungi? Who considers that by felling old trees and replacing them with foreign species many species of mychorriza are doomed? Not even conservation areas which are famous for their wealth of rare fungi, are safe from the forester's saw. The fears that with the destruction of forests which can be seen all around us, a large part of the local fungal flora may be threatened by extinction has to be taken extremely seriously. There is no doubt that as trees disappear, the fungal species connected with them disappear too. Many mycologists believe that they have already observed changes in the fungal flora as a consequence of acid rain. However, as it is not possible to predict the fruiting of certain fungi, such conclusions have to be regarded with caution. The evidence that damage to forests has an impact on some fungus species is not conclusive as yet. Should the forests disappear, a possibility in the next few decades, an ecological catastrophe of unimaginable proportion would ensue. There are, however, probably many worse consequences of the ultimate destruction of the natural landscape, for our climate and water supplies, for example, than the extinction of our fungal flora.

Advice for the fungi collector

Up to 90% of each fungus consists of water. The dry substance contains mainly protein, carbohydrates, vitamins and a negligible amount of fat.

Ground rules

1) When collecting fungi to eat, only take those which you can identify with certainty.
2) Cut fungi off carefully, or twist them off; close the hole left in the soil and clean the fungi where you found them.
3) Transport fungi in airy containers; never use plastic bags, only paper ones.
4) Keep fungi to be eaten separate from any fungus specimen which you cannot identify with certainty and which you want to look at at home; collect the whole fungus and transport it in a separate container.

Freezing mushrooms

Only species with firm flesh which are freshly picked are suitable for freezing. They must be cleaned and sliced (prepared for cooking) before being frozen. Fungi must be frozen fast and they can then be kept frozen for 6 months. This period can be slightly extended, and space saved, by briefly par-boiling the fungi then giving them a quick cold rinse, but some of the taste will be lost in this way. The fungi must not be thawed before use, but must be cooked, fried or stewed from frozen.

Drying mushrooms

Only species with firm flesh, collected in the dry state can be dried; tube fungi are among the most suitable. For drying in air the fungi should be sliced thinly, threaded and suspended in a well-aired, warm room.

Alternatively the sliced mushrooms can be dried in the oven in approximately 24 hours. The temperature setting for this should be 50°c or 120-125°F, a cool oven. The door has to be kept slightly ajar. Turning the slices after about 12 hours prevents them from sticking to the shelf.

Growing your own mushrooms

Some fungal species like the champignons (*Agaricus campestris*) and the oyster mushroom (*Pleurotus ostreatus*) are sometimes offered in a kit to grow at home. They are not the most palatable fungi, but if the directions are observed carefully good harvests can be achieved. However, this is best looked upon as a hobby rather than a source of income. Sometimes the kit may be infected with other fungal spores which then give rise to fungal 'weeds' instead of the edible mushrooms that were expected. Such weeds must, of course, not be eaten.

Mushrooms recommended for eating which can be easily identified

N°, Latin name	Common name	Season found	Uses
1, *Boletus edulis*	Penny-bun	summer–autumn	suitable for all purposes, also drying
15, *Xerocomus badius*	Bay Boletus	autumn	as Penny-bun
33, *Leccinum scabrum*	Brown Birch Bolete	summer–autumn	cooking not drying
36, *Leccinum versipelle*	Orange Birch Bolete	summer–autumn	as Brown Birch Bolete
155, *Macrolepiota procera*	Parasol mushroom	summer–autumn	as vegetable; caps can be fried
206, *Coprinus comatus*	Shaggy Ink Cap	summer–autumn	for all purposes, except drying
300, *Lactarius volemus*	(none)	summer–autumn	frying only
381, *Morchella esculenta*	Common Morel	spring	vegetable, sauce
348, *Cantharellus cibarius*	Chanterelle	summer–autumn	seasoning, soups, as vegetable, not for drying

Glossary

Acuminate: tapering into a sharp point
Areolate: sunken areas on surface, rectangular to polygonal
Ascomycetes: group of fungi with spores in spore sac (= ascus)
Basidiomycetes: group of fungi with spores budding from basidia
Contorted: bent or twisted
Deliquescent: tissue gradually dissolving
Denticulate: finely serrate (see ends)
Felted: dense felt formed by minute hairs of fibres
Fibrous: compaction of fibres
Flooci: patches of remnants of universal veil or other wart-like irregularities of surface (floccose: with minute flocci)
Fruit body: entire mushroom, flesh and fertile layer of tubes or gills
Fruit layer: fertile layer alone, which is not structured by tubes or gills
Gleba: central mass of spore-producing tissue in gasteromycetes
Heart wood: water-conducting central part of tree
Hyphae: any of the filaments that constitute the fungal body (mycelium)
Mealy: smelling or tasting of flour or dough
Milk: liquid released by some fungi when damaged
Minutely: finely
Pruinose: with a bloom (often white, but not necessarily so)
Pulvinate: cushion like
Sclerotium: firm mass of hyphae: a non-growing stage for fungus
Tuberous: shape reminiscent of a potato or other bulbous growth
Umbo: raised centre of cap

Mushrooms and toadstools

The terms mushroom and toadstool are common names referring in the main to fungi from the orders Agaricales, Russulales and Boletales. The fruit bodies of these have clearly defined cap and stem. In the English language the implication is that mushrooms are edible and toadstools are poisonous. The names can be misleading though, and there are a number of poisonous 'mushrooms'.

The word mushroom appears to have its roots in the old French term mousseron from mousse meaning moss, implying that a mushroom's habitat is 'among moss'. The word toadstool contains all the dark suspicions of poison and evil, that in medieval times were connected with the sadly maligned toad.

The scope of *Collins Nature Guide to Mushrooms and Toadstools* is very much wider than the title suggests. We cover all forms of fungus, from the easily recognizable cap fungi, to bracket fungi, coral fungi, polypores, and many other interesting forms. We have therefore decided to refer to all of them within the book as fungi.

Species Index

The figures indicate page numbers
[f. = forma or variety]